Finding out about finding out:
a practical guide to
children's information books

Finding out about Finding out

A PRACTICAL GUIDE TO CHILDREN'S INFORMATION BOOKS

Bobbie Neate

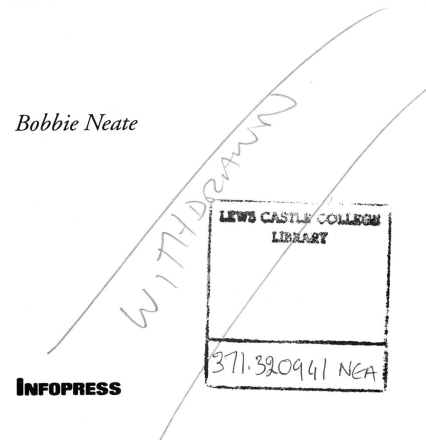

INFOPRESS

Copyright © Bobbie Neate 1992
Published in 1999 by Infopress
Hedgerows
33 Downside Road
Winchester
SO22 5LT

First published in 1992 by Hodder & Stoughton

ISBN 0 9535642 0 7

British Library Cataloguing in Publication Data
A catalogue record for this book is available from the British
Library

This book production has been managed by Amolibros
Printed and bound by Professional Book Supplies, Oxford,
England

I would like to dedicate this book to my three young children Tom, Rupert and Hannah who will I hope, in future years, gain expertise in the field of 'reading to learn', from an enlightened teacher.

Publisher's acknowledgments

The publishers would like to thank the following for permission to reproduce material in this volume:

B. T. Batsford Ltd; A&C Black; Blackwell Scientific Publishers Ltd; Cambridge University Press; Center for the Study of Reading (Urbana, USA); Department of Education and Science; Professor Margaret Donaldson; Employment Department for Manpower Services Commission material; Falmer Press; The *Guardian*; HMSO, for material reproduced with permission of the controller of Her Majesty's Stationery Office; International Reading Association; Ladybird Books Ltd; Landsforeningen af Laesepaedagogen; Longman Group UK; The Lutterworth Press; A. Morris and N. Stewart-Dore; National Curriculum Council; National Trust; The Open University; Oxford University Press; Penguin Books Ltd; P.S.R.D.G.; The Publishers Association; Rand McNally; *The Times*; The United Kingdom Reading Association.

The publishers would also like to acknowledge the following for use of their material:

Academic Press (USA); Addison–Wesley Publishers; HarperCollins Publishers; Heinemann Educational Books Ltd; Holt Rinehart and Winston Ltd; Lawrence Erlbaum Associates Inc.; Methuen Children's Books; Mills and Boon (Publishers) Ltd; Prentice–Hall Inc; Simon and Schuster Young Books; Franklin Watts; Wayland (Publishers) Ltd.

Infopress has made every effort to trace copyright holders for all previously published copyright material, and believes it has done so, but if copyright holders wish to contact Infopress they should do so at the publisher's address.

Contents

Note   Throughout this book there are activities for the reader. The reader is requested to pause after reading each initial instruction, before proceeding onto the body of the activity. This time for reflection will ensure the reader gains maximum benefit from the activities.

Author's acknowledgments

I would like to thank my children, my colleagues and all the teachers who have attended my Inset courses. Eleven institutions have greatly contributed to my way of thinking and provided me with valuable information on how children acquire the skill of reading to learn. They are:
Harry Gosling Junior School
Gordon Junior School
Nightingale School
De Lucy School
Canon Barnett School
Ruxley Manor School
Linton Meads School
Greenwich Professional Centre
St Peter's School
Wyborne Junior School
Torridon School
I would also like to thank all my friends for being so supportive and for showing interest in my studies. I would particularly like to thank Margaret Hamer who found time to read my draft with great care, enthusiasm and energy, Michael Goldman who gave valuable support and guidance and Janet Palmer who commented helpfully on the script.

Advance organiser

This book is aimed at the teacher, adviser, librarian, psychologist or anybody who works with primary aged children, for it is with the very young that work on informative reading must start, as will be shown throughout the book. However, the emphasis on young children's reading does not rule out the usefulness of this book to those teaching in the secondary sector. All the activities suggested are appropriate to any age level, and very often the same project books are used in both sectors of education.

This book can be read in many ways and the way you tackle it should depend on what you want to find out. You might find that you get more out of the book by setting up your own questions. Ask yourself what you want to know about children's 'finding out' skills, then make up some more specific questions. You should then read the book so that you are looking for answers to your questions.

You could reasonably read the chapters in any order, but to get a real understanding of all the issues involved, you should at least skim the whole book so that you obtain a picture of the mismatch between the task (how to read to learn) and the tools (children's books). It is my belief that if you are a teacher wishing to improve your children's notemaking skills, you should read the whole book, not just the last chapter, because statements made in that chapter are dependent on what has been written before.

In some chapters I have included activities for you to try. You may find these irritating because your reading is being held up. I have included them for two reasons: one is because some of my arguments are best explained by the activities; the other is because you are more likely to understand the issues involved if I encourage you to become engaged with the text. I have designed the activities, however, so that they can be left out and returned to later, according to your own preference.

A list of definitions has been included in the book for those readers who are not familiar with linguistic terms and those words which have a specific meaning within the study of reading.

In this book you will be reading about the following.

1   The basic difficulty children have with 'finding out'. There are two

parts to this: one is reading to learn and the other is finding the relevant material within a book.

2   The three basic reasons why children find informative reading hard.

3   My own view of reading (Chapters 1 and 2), and why the task of reading for information should be approached differently from children's normal story reading.

4   The diversity of children's information books (Chapters 3, 4, 5, 6).

5   The problems children have with finding material within books, and why teaching children traditional study skills is sometimes problematic (Chapter 3).

6   The difficulty of children's books according to readability formulae (Chapter 4).

7   The variety of language found in the texts, from which children are expected to learn (Chapters 5 and 6). Chapter 5 explains why there is diversity and Chapter 6 gives examples of text from various books.

8   In Chapter 7 you will find the first part of the book summarised and discussion of some of the issues which arise. You might also want to refer to Chapter 7 for the author's recommendations and suggestions about improving the quality of children's books before you read anything else.

9   In Chapter 8 you will learn methods of teaching children to survey books, to set up good questions, and how to really read for meaning. A number of different strategies are explained which enable children to become effective notemakers.

When you have retrieved the content, thought about the concepts and thoroughly interacted with the views expressed in this book, I hope you will hurry to your children's bookshelves, read some of the books on display and then understand the enormity of the task your children face when asked to 'find out'. I also hope to have given you enough ideas and suggestions to help children develop their informative reading. If they learn the art of 'finding out' in the primary school, it will be a skill for life.

Definitions of technical terms used

Cline

This term was first used in Hallidayan Linguistics and refers to a continuum upon which texts can be positioned according to their features. As with any continuum there are clear differences between the extremes, but the changes are gradual as you move along the cline. The categories within the cline are not distinct but shade into each other. It is impossible to tell where one ends and the next begins.

Very often, items are positioned on a continuum by 'feel' rather than exact science. In my study, items were put into different categories along the cline according to the feel of the language rather than because they fulfilled any particular formal requirements.

In this study, a cline is a scale with a number of definite points. Each point can be identified but the beginnings and ends blur into each other. The items in each category on the cline do not all match one criterion but they are more similar to, than different from, each other.

This term is of particular help in the area of literary studies dealt with in this book because it enables one to assess the formality of the registers of the text.

Cohesion

Cohesion is a device in texts. It is what makes a text a text.

Cohesion depends on devices which link together parts of a text. These may be backward or forward links. These devices are called cohesive ties. Pronouns are one example of cohesive ties: they stand for the nouns that they replace. These nouns have already been introduced in the text. Thus, in the example *David put his coat on. He had taken it off because of the heat coming from the fire.* 'He' is referring to David. We know from the pronoun that David is the person in question. If 'David' had been repeated it would have been less clear who the person was: *David put his coat on. David had taken it off because of the heat coming from the fire.* Similarly 'it' in the second sentence refers to 'coat' in the first sentence. Cohesion helps the reader to understand a text, but it is also thought that cohesive ties in text are difficult for young children to use and understand.

Connectives

These are ties that link one sentence with a preceding one. Examples of simple connectives are *and*, *but*. Examples of connectives that are thought to be more difficult for children are *nevertheless*, *however*, and *additionally*.

Concept overload

This phrase describes texts that give a large body of knowledge to the reader in a small number of words. There is little redundancy (see **redundancy**).

Ellipsis

Ellipsis occurs when something of structural necessity has been missed out of a text. It does not mean that the text cannot be understood: the text may have an incompleteness associated with it. For instance *Herons are unusual birds. However there are quite a few * * around here* (* * ellipsis). In this example *of them* or *herons* is missed out of the second sentence. Ellipsis is believed to make texts more difficult for young children.

Embedding

Embedding is the inclusion of one sentence within another or of a relative clause in a noun phrase such as *The man, who has a beard, walked along the road*. Embedding is believed to make texts more difficult for young children.

Expository text

This refers to text that is informational in nature.

Field

Field is one of the three elements, with **mode** and **tenor**, that make up **register**. Field is the *content* of what is going on in a text. It provides the specialist words and sets the scene in a text. Each subject area, such as Geography, has field words such as ridge, escarpement, plateau.

Narrative text

This refers to text that follows a story line (see **story grammar**).

Mode

This is one of the features of **register**. Mode changes according to the channel of communication. For instance, the differences between spoken and written language are made by mode. Mode puts the context into language. In written situations more context is required than in oral situations. For instance, the commentary on a tennis match on the radio or television is very different. The radio commentator has to fill in the context for the listener. One of the reasons that children find writing difficult is that they are unfamiliar with this 'mode'.

Prior knowledge

Prior knowledge is thought to help the reader a great deal when reading an unfamiliar expository text. Prior knowledge is thought to be of more importance in expository texts than narrative texts. The term is used to define what a reader already knows before he/she tries reading a text. Chapman (1984) sees prior knowledge being divided into three elements. The text bound, the context bound, and the real world.

The real world element is probably most lacking in primary aged children, who obviously have less experience of the world than adults. It is not just that they lack specific knowledge but also that they have not experienced so much of life.

Another element is the text bound: young children have not been reading as long as adults so they lack the knowledge of books. They may have been reading narrative texts and therefore do not know the conventions of information books. For instance the layout is different in this type of book.

Finally the context bound is interesting because this is knowledge that is expected of the reader by the writer. For instance, *what do you know about the causes of the Second World War?* Readers would start from different knowledge bases according to their age, their possible position in the war, and their interest in the subject.

Psycholinguist

A person who brings together the fields of psychology and linguistics.

Readability

Readability is an assessment of the features of a text that make one text easier to read than another. There are many features of a text that affect the ease with which it is read. Texts with a high readability are more difficult than those with a low readability.

Readability Formulae

These are formulae designed to measure the readability of texts. They are usually based on the number of words in each sentence and the number of difficult words within the text. A text with many unusual words and a high average sentence length will be assigned a higher readability level than a text that has fewer unusual words and shorter sentences.

Redundancy

This occurs when an author uses essentially the same information in more than one form, in other words a large number of words is used to explain a simple message. It is thought that a certain amount of redundancy or apparently unnecessary repetition can help readers on information texts, because they reduce the **concept load**.

Register

This is language variously used, according to situations. Language, whether it is spoken or written, changes according to circumstances and whom the writer or speaker is addressing. In oral situations we change our vocabulary and sentence structure according to whom we are talking. The same goes for written language, the writer selects the words and grammatical structure that they think will suit their readers best.

Some authors want to keep their distance from the reader. They want to impose their social distance on the reader and the writer can do this by using specialist terms and formal language. This is called formal register. However, other authors design texts that will welcome the lay reader. The writers may write within the range of words that they think the reader will understand. They might explain more terms than the formal writer would. The author might be at pains not to create a social distance between the reader and him/herself. This is called informal register. Register is made of three parts: field, mode and tenor.

Story Grammar

Story Grammar is the convention of a narrative text. Each story or narrative has a start, which might be a setting of the scene or an introduction to the characters. This is followed by a dramatic occurrence, which is either resolved or not during the course of the text. Each narrative has a beginning, an event, and a resolution.

Structural Guiders

This term applies to those features of an informational text that help readers to find the information they seek. In this book they cover bibliographies, indexes, glossaries, references to illustrations, introductions, contents pages, cover blurbs, summaries and headings.

Tenor

Tenor is the third of the features that make up **register**. It refers to social distance between author and reader. Some authors make themselves more remote than others: some will not make themselves known to the reader, while others will frequently use the pronominal 'I'.

Introduction

A CATALOGUE OF FAILURE

My first real experience of utter failure and a complete sense of hopelessness in the classroom occurred when I tried to teach my first class of 7 and 8 year-olds how to retrieve information from their collection of project books. I can remember how enthusiastic I was as a keen young teacher that the children should be able to pursue their own line of enquiry and learn from the texts. I can also recall how dispirited I felt when I found that my pupils were unable to do so. There seemed to be a number of reasons for their failure and I tried to remedy these.

First, I found that the children could not find the information that they wanted. They could not find the right books, and once they had retrieved them they did not know their way around them. A major problem was that the children did not really know how to ask questions from the books. For instance they might suggest a global question such as 'to find out about dinosaurs'. So they would get a book on dinosaurs, and because the whole of the books was about their topic they would then proceed to copy it out: all of the information in the book was relevant! The pupils had failed to be selective and had often failed to see the point of making parts of the text redundant. All of the children copied in one way or another. The more able children left out certain words or sentences, but they rarely tried to reorganise the original text.

So I decided I would teach my pupils study skills – it seemed that the children did not know how to use the library nor did they know how to use information books. So I went through the traditional library skills with them and then tried to teach them how to use the structural guiders in a non-fiction book. During the course of my lessons I began to realise just how difficult these skills were for children, and just how laborious they found them. It was at this stage that I really started to notice how weak the information books themselves seemed to be. Having noticed the difficulties I nevertheless continued to pursue my goal.

I also tried to tackle the tendency to copy. I looked for literature on the subject and found very little, but I remember how I had been taught as a child and I tried to reapply it. I tried two basic strategies. First I taught the children to read the text, close the book, remember what the text was about and then write it down. Second, I told the children to change the author's words into their own.

Neither of these two strategies worked. I realised that the former strategy was not a notemaking technique at all, but a memory test. The second was a very demanding task because authors have usually chosen the best words and have had the freedom to put them in any order. The notemaker has to choose words of similar meaning and to alter the order of presentation. This is a very difficult job for an adult, and even more so for a child.

Despite the problems we had encountered, I still expected a great improvement in the children's work. However, to my horror, the pupils seemed to be doing no better. In fact, they seemed now to lack confidence. They could find the relevant book a little more quickly but they often seemed unable to find a relevant piece of text. Although I had tried to teach them to use the structural guiders, they did not seem to be using them. They still seemed to be copying material almost directly from the books and, most worryingly, they did not seem to understand what they had read. Nevertheless, I was not to be defeated, and I resolved to look into this matter in more depth.

I started in a small way, but when an opportunity arose to study for a research degree I decided that informative reading for young children was to be the focus of my study. My early research work seemed so unsuccessful that at one stage I began to wonder whether the skill of searching for information, interacting with the text and then reorganising it in the form of notes, was in fact too hard conceptually for this age-group. Children could often read a text out loud to me but it seemed as if they could not interpret it. They certainly did not seem to learn anything of significance from it.

During the early stages of the research I found that I was not alone with my problems. All the difficulties I was having were well documented, but the literature was very weak on remedies. My research went in two directions. First the book themselves were analysed according to three criteria. Second, methods were devised to help very young children with research skills. It turned out to be a fascinating study, and one that still intrigues me. I will give a synopsis of my work here, because all my early judgements of the books proved to be correct. However, my concerns about the children's abilities proved to be unfounded. The failure was in the nature of the tools I had been giving to the children, not in their abilities.

Findings about the books

- The books did not have enough good quality structural guiders for them to be of value to the children.
- The books were either too hard or too simplistic for the children to be able to extract any real information.
- The books were often poorly organised.
- Information books seemed to be the Cinderella of the children's book trade, and the whole approach to their production needed to be thoroughly overhauled.

Findings about the children

The young children with whom I worked could be taught to be selective and they were able to develop flexible reading habits. If they were given strategies which helped them to interact with text and make parts of it redundant, then they became effective notemakers and were able, even at a very young age, to learn from texts.

1 Reading for pleasure or for information

"Miss Beale said you would show me round to look at the projects" said Andrew.
"Why, do you want to copy one?" asked Victor . . . "You could copy mine only someone might recognise it. I've done that three times already. Twice in the Junior school and now I'm doing it again."
(Mark, 1976)

This chapter is designed to help you to think about and perhaps reassess what you see reading to be. Your understanding of the process will I hope be heightened by carrying out the activities provided, before reading on.

I start with a discussion on reading; I pursue the subject of reading for information and, as a result of the evidence, I then suggest that children ought to be taught flexible reading strategies during their early schooling. The type of reading required for project work is then addressed. This is followed in Chapter 2 by a discussion on books, their value, their place in school and the problems that they create. A major part of the chapter describes the differences between the two types of book – narrative and expository.

READING

Activity 1

What is reading?
Jot down your own ideas about what reading is.
If possible, discuss with somebody else the notes you have made before looking to see what I have written.

There is no single right answer to the question 'What is reading?' for there are many interpretations of the word. In fact most of my argument during the first half of the chapter hangs on the fact that there is no consensus of views about the definition of 'reading'. Furthermore, the main area of contention is that of comprehension. Does the term 'reading' involve understanding or not? Some educationalists and psychologists are happy to define reading as decoding of print. In other words, reading occurs when the reader pronounces the words in a text either aloud or in their heads. They are responding to the graphic signals. However, others are not happy with this type of definition because they feel that a further response is required from the reader: they need to be able to respond to the meaning as well as to the graphic signals.

Some educationalists and psychologists will go further and insist that reading involves the reader not only responding to the meaning but also evaluating the message behind it and comparing this with their previous experiences or thoughts on the matter.

There are thus three levels of reading expected in these three definitions of the term: decoding, responding and interpreting. The dictionary definition of reading is ". . . the activity of looking at written or printed symbols and pronouncing them". By contrast, Kenneth Goodman, an American psycholinguist, sees reading as being on one level, but more than just decoding of print. He sees reading as:

> . . . a smooth, rapid guessing game in which the reader samples from available language cues, using the least amount of available information to achieve this essential task of reconstructing and comprehending the writer's meaning. It can be regarded as a systematic reduction of uncertainty as the reader starts with the graphic input and ends with meaning.
> (Goodman, 1976)

Nevertheless, Jonathan Anderson, an Australian reading authority, does pursue the three levels idea. He compares reading to the performance of a symphony orchestra:

> This analogy illustrates three points. First, like the performance of a symphony, reading is a holistic act. In other words, while reading can be analysed into sub-skills such as discriminating letters and identifying words, performing the sub-skills one at a time does not constitute reading. Reading can be said to take place only when the parts are put together in a smooth integrated performance. Second, success in reading comes from practise over long periods of time, like skill in playing musical instruments. Indeed, it is a lifelong endeavour. Third, as with a musical score, there may be more than one interpretation of

a text. The integration depends on the background of the reader, the purpose for reading, and the context in which reading occurs.
(Anderson, 1983)

I do not think it is prudent here to pursue further the discussion of what reading entails. However, I do think it must be made clear what my own views are. I cannot myself accept that reading can be just pronouncing the words on a page. It must involve comprehending. In my view, people who just voice the words are not really reading. The definition that I think is most appropriate to this book is that of the Danish authority Morgens Jansen:

The distinction between reading and comprehending is merely semantic because without comprehension reading is just following the marks on the page.
(Jansen, M., 1987, written in English)

I also like the clever analogy of Samuel Coleridge who sees reading in terms of the reader. He identifies four classes of reader:

1 Sponges who absorb all they read and return it nearly in the same state only a little dirtied;

2 Sand glasses, who retain nothing and are content to get through a book for the sake of getting through the time;

3 Strain bags, who merely retain the dregs of what they read;

4 Mogul diamonds, equally rare as the diamond, who profit by what they read, and enable others to profit also.
(Samuel Taylor Coleridge in Notebooks as quoted by Merritt and Prior (eds), 1977)

I find these classes of readers rather depressing, because all too often in my experience both adults and children fall into the first three categories if they are not given specific help in their early years. There have been great discussions in the popular press recently on standards of reading. In my view, these arguments are to some extent red herrings, because what is important is whether readers can match their reading to their reading purpose. It is not enough to assess whether someone can or cannot read a certain text aloud.

In the words of Thornton:

... we should be less concerned with simplistic questions of whether pupils can or cannot read but rather with what they can or cannot do with their reading ability and why.
(Thornton, 1986)

We must teach children from the earliest years that reading involves looking for the meaning behind the words on the page. If they do this, they are deep readers; if they only read the words then they are surface readers.

COMPREHENSION

I have already mentioned 'comprehension' but I would like the reader of this book to now think about what the word means to them.

Activity 2

What is comprehension?
Throughout this book I will be emphasising the importance of children comprehending the words that they see on the page. Reading without comprehension is a meaningless activity. Reading must involve understanding.

Reading is an activity that takes place in the head. We can watch children read but we can only guess from their outward activities whether they have understood or not. We cannot see the comprehending process. I take the view that, in order to comprehend, the reader must conduct a mental dialogue with the absent writer. The reader is predicting, formulating, and testing hypotheses; the words on the page either confirm or oppose the reader's views.

However, like the various theories suggested on 'what is reading?' there is no one model which answers the question 'what is comprehension?' Basically there are two models, one is known as the 'new' model while the other is becoming known as the 'old'.

The 'old' model consisted of a reader working on a text and producing an output that was either right or wrong. I am referring to the standard comprehension exercises in which the child was asked to read a text and then answer questions, such as the one shown opposite.

A coat of arms and the surrounding parts is called an achievement of arms and consists of up to seven parts: shield, helmet, wreath, crest, mantling, motto and supporters. The helmet rests on top of the shield, except when the coat of arms belongs to a peer. (A peer has a coronet above the shield and the helmet is placed above the coronet.) The wreath fits round the top of the helmet and just below the crest. The mantling is an array of ornamental drapery around the shield. The motto, written on a scroll, is usually found below the shield. Supporters, if any, are usually placed one on each side of the shield.

What name is given to a coat of arms and its surrounding parts?
Where does the helmet rest?
Where does the wreath fit?
What is the mantling?

The output was usually in the form of written exercises. The model was that the reader either comprehended or did not comprehend, it was a 'once-and-for-all' affair. It was thought that children could either do comprehension exercises or they could not.

As a result of this type of work the 'New' model of comprehension has emerged. The New model sees comprehension as an ever-more-precise process of emergent understanding. This view of comprehension places much emphasis on the importance of prior knowledge to the reader's understanding. We do not understand all texts to the same level. One text is easier for us than another. As Chapman (1984) says, readers who are brilliant scholars in Botany may have considerable if not extreme difficulty with a text on Nuclear Physics, if they have no previous experience of that area of Physics.

There are some texts, presenting issues on which we have a great deal of previous knowledge or situations of which we have experience, that we are more likely to comprehend at a much higher level than texts whose subjects are unfamiliar to us. John Chapman sees the model as a continuum, as illustrated in figure 1.1 below.

We move backwards and forwards across the model according to our prior knowledge of its content and text type. We might be at level one when reading a text on a subject of which we have little prior knowledge, but at the same time be at level four when reading a text that is about our hobby. Our reading efficiency depends on whether we know a lot about the subject involved and whether we have sufficient conceptual hooks on which to peg our thoughts.

However the difficulty of the text or the newness of its subject to us are not our only problems. We also experience the 'bedtime reading syndrome' when our minds are not reading the text attentively enough. In many situations we know we have 'read' the page – the words have passed in front of our eyes. Even so, when we get to the bottom of the page we realise that we have absorbed nothing. Sometimes we can even remember the words but not what the message in the text was. This is not real or 'deep' reading.

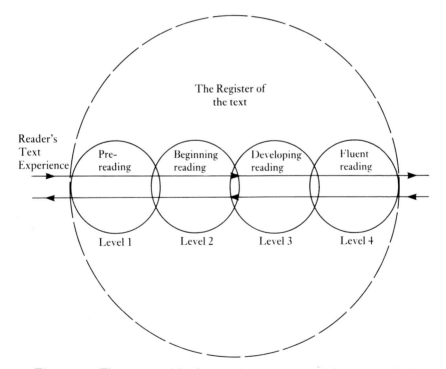

Fig. 1.1   The new model of comprehension (adapted from a model by J. Chapman)

Often it is a result of the reader not having sufficient knowledge on which to base interactions with the text.

Activity 3

Think seriously, remembering the points I have just made, about the following simple question.

Can you read?

Well, can you?

Now think about the following questions and try the activities.
Can you read the three texts below?

THE MYTH OF THE AESTHETIC ATTITUDE

Some recent articles[1] have suggested the unsatisfactoriness of the notion of the aesthetic attitude and it is now time for a fresh look at that encrusted article of faith. This conception has been valuable to aesthetics and criticism in helping wean them from a sole concern with beauty and related notions.[2] However, I shall argue that the aesthetic attitude is a myth and while, as G. Ryle has said, "Myths often do a lot of theoretical good while they are still new."[3] this particular one is no longer useful and in fact misleads aesthetic theory.

There is a range of theories which differ according to how strongly the aesthetic attitude is characterized. This variation is reflected in the language the theories employ. The strongest variety is Edward Bullough's theory of psychical distance, recently defended by Sheila Dawson.[4] The central technical term of this theory is "distance" used as a verb to denote an action which either constitutes or is necessary for the aesthetic attitude. These theorists use such sentences as "He distanced (or failed to distance) the play." The second variety is widely held but has been defended most vigorously in recent years by Jerome Stolnitz and Eliseo Vivas. The central technical term of this variety is "disinterested"[5] used either as an adverb or as an adjective.

(Hegel, 1975)

A CASE FOR A ALIEN ANCESTRY?

MATCHING A GENETIC MATERIAL TO AN ENVIRONMENT

We can see the phenotype of a modern organism as a specific disturbance in the environment produced by a set of DNA base sequences. The special problem of the origin of life arises because

DNA, at least in our present environment, requires an exceedingly elaborate pre-existing disturbance not only to replicate efficiently but to replicate at all. In this sense DNA is badly matched to our general environments. It is like a traveller from an alien world who must carry with him essential and complex life support systems. And herein lies the paradox of the origin of life: how did the support systems arise in the first place? The usual way of trying to resolve this paradox is by supposing that there was a situation on earth in the remote past when DNA or something like it, was more at home – where the support systems were not initially required. It is supposed that there used to be a non-biological matched environment for DNA.

As indicated in the earlier discussion I am inclined to think that there was never a non-biological matched environment for any nucleic acid-like molecules, that these are essentially sophisticated genetic materials: like magnetic tape, they can be a very efficient means of handling information but they are necessarily committed to pre-existing complex machinery: in nature they are matched only to an environment that consists of the interior of a well-equipped cell. (Bligh, Cloudsley, Thompson, Macdonald, 1976)

Materia Medica

From such a materia medica everything that is conjectural, all that is mere assertion or imaginary should be strictly excluded; everything should be the pure language of nature carefully and honestly interrogated.

Of a truth, it is only by a very considerable store of medicines accurately known in respect of these their pure modes of action in altering the health of man, that we can be placed in a position to discover a homœopathic remedy, a suitable artificial (curative) morbific analogue for *each* of infinitely numerous morbid states in nature, for *every* malady in the world.[1] In the meantime, even now – thanks to the truthful character of the symptoms,[a] and to the abundance of disease elements which every one of the powerful medicinal substances has already shown in its action on the healthy body – but few diseases remain, for which a tolerably suitable homœopathic remedy may not be met with among those now proved as to their pure action,[2] which, without much disturbance, restores health in a gentle, sure and permanent manner – *infinitely* more surely and safely than can be effected by all the general and special

therapeutics of the old allopathic medical art with its un-
known composite remedies, which do but alter and aggra-
vate but cannot cure chronic diseases, and rather retard
than promote recovery from acute diseases.[a]*
  * [These are added after 'acute diseases' in the Sixth
Edition: "and frequently endanger life."]
(Hahnemann, 1952)

Which text do you think is easier?
Why do you think this?

I hope that carrying out these activities will have alerted you further to what
reading really is: it is likely that at least one of the texts is on a topic with
which you are not familiar. On this unfamiliar topic, what did you find that
your brain was doing?

When I have set up similar reading activities in workshops I have received
comments from the participants with which you might feel you can identify.
For instance, many readers have reacted emotionally and suggested that they
were worried, anxious, or wanted to shout 'help' because they felt
inadequate; others suggested that they felt bored, rebellious or resentful.
Some wanted to shout 'Why do I have to read this? What's the point?'. In your
situation you may have just not bothered to read the text at all.

When I have asked participants about the reading process, many of them
have realised that they were reading the words, but were not deep reading.
They could pronounce the words but they could not tell their partners what
the text was about. Some experienced the 'bedtime reading syndrome':
they were looking at the words but their minds were on other things.

Some adults, when faced with a hard text, try to read the text really slowly
to understand one sentence, then tackle another. However, in this
laborious process they often find themselves losing track of the whole text.
Other adults might read the whole text quickly to get the gist of the subject
and then return to analyse the parts. Some readers find themselves reading,
and then re-reading, but still not understanding. Most adult readers will
admit that they experience a cut-off point. The material gets too hard for
them: they have no conceptual background, no hooks on which to peg the
ideas, and finally they give up.

I would like to return now to the question 'What is reading?'. Which of
the texts were you able to read? You probably found one text easier than the
others. Can you put this down to the fact that you knew more about that
topic?

I think that the importance of prior knowledge has really been under-
played when it comes to children's reading. As will be seen later in the

chapter, each time children start a new topic they are being put into a situation in which their lack of prior knowledge hinders their reading. They do not have sufficient conceptual hooks when they start a project. It is now realised that the process of comprehension is that of 'building bridges'. It is the building of bridges between the new information in the text and information previously known by the reader. It is similar to problem solving and, in my view, children must be able to build bridges and problem-solve if they are going to learn properly from informative texts.

From my work in primary schools, I suspect that what often passes as reading of informative books is not really reading at all, but merely a passing of words in front of the eyes. Many primary pupils are using reading habits similar to those of the secondary pupils in Lunzer and Gardner's study (1979) which found that the children were not reading for meaning (this work is referred to in greater depth later in the chapter). The findings of the APU (APU/DES, 1982) were similar.

The recent work of Chapman suggests that there is a basic level of background knowledge that is necessary for the process of understanding:

> . . . it is possible that there is a threshold of prior knowledge required for the reader to learn efficiently from the text.
> (Chapman, 1984)

One of the major problems, as will be seen later, is that some authors assume that their young readers have more basic knowledge than, in fact, they do. It is now recognised that children bring to school stores of knowledge that differ considerably in amount, kind and quantity. Often teachers, as adults, do not realise that their prior knowledge differs markedly from that of their pupils. This may be because of their home environment or it may be because adults and children have had different experiences.

I have argued that comprehension is not now seen as a once-and-for-all matter, and that one of the reasons for this is that we read texts according to how much prior knowledge we have on the subject. This prior knowledge is of increased importance when it comes to expository texts, because it is with informational reading that the reader's background experiences are more likely to be varied. One of the reasons that children find expository reading difficult could well be that they do not have such a wide experience of life as adults do, and they thus lack the necessary background knowledge for many types of text.

Let us now think in more depth about reading for information.

Activity 4

What is reading for information?
Is reading for information the same as reading?

There is relatively little literature available on informational reading but I suggest that the term informational reading implies that there must be understanding (Spiro, 1980; Sanford and Garrod, 1981; Otto and White, 1982). It is more than just reading. If one is reading for information then some new information must be obtained from the process. When reading for information, readers are probably reading about something new, something they did not know about before. The term informational reading also suggests that the reading tends to be selective. The reader will probably use a different reading strategy from that used on a novel.

It is appropriate here to consider the different reading strategies that make up the skills of a flexible reader.

READING STRATEGIES

To read a narrative text there is one basic reading approach. The reader selects the book by surveying the cover, reading the blurb and perhaps selectively reading odd parts of the text. Then, the reader will generally proceed by starting from page one, and continuing onwards towards the back of the book. Narrative texts are encouraging: the author pulls us along and we want to know what is going to happen next. A narrative text usually has several climaxes. Unless the novel is of a very demanding nature, or we are formally studying the text, we read almost passively, or in the words of Coleridge, we 'soak up' the storyline. However, as will be seen later, to read for learning we should be active readers searching the text for answers to our questions. Information books have their own characteristics – they are not necessarily 'a good read', that is, they are not usually exciting or encouraging to the reader. On the other hand, information books do have other strengths. They tell us about things we want to know, or perhaps things we knew little about. They build on our existing knowledge and extend it. They inspire us to look elsewhere to further this knowledge. They are, by their very nature and purpose, different from narrative texts.

There are three possible reading strategies for reading information books, depending on the reader's purpose. The first is to get the general gist of a text: to read so that one gets a preview of the text, perhaps by finding the summary or introduction. Not all of the text is read. This is often called skimming.

A second strategy is to read the text for one or two specific facts. The reader would have a specific question in mind and would then scan the text to find an answer to it. The answer might consist of a date, a number, or a list of items. The third strategy is to read a piece of text in detail. This is often called intensive reading. Some readers will use this strategy to analyse a text on a subject with which they are not familiar: in this case they find the understanding part of the process more difficult. Alternatively, the readers might be students of that subject and really have to learn and understand the material in detail.

Lunzer and Gardner (1979) identified three types of reading going on in schools. They called them *rejective, reflective* and *receptive*. The term 'receptive reading' is reserved for situations where the author is pulling the reader along. Readers do not need to tax their brains because the text is well within their capabilities. The written material is based on the readers' prior experience. Readers probably find themselves sharing experiences with the writer. This receptive reading therefore occurs most often on narrative texts.

'Reflective reading' occurs when the reader thinks in depth about the text. The reflective reader may not read the text from beginning to end, as in receptive reading, but read a sentence or paragraph and then reflect, perhaps by moving the eyes away from the text or perhaps by directing the eyes back to an earlier section. The eyes probably dart about the text. It is not a straight read. This type of reading strategy is more likely on an expository text, for the material is likely to be new to the reader. The reflective approach is usually used by a reader who has some background knowledge of the subject but is not an expert. The text, even so, should demand that the reader reflects.

'Rejective reading' occurs when readers have so little background knowledge of a particular text or subject, and find so many pieces of information or concepts of which they have not had experience, that they fail to achieve any real understanding. Often one familiar word used in a specialist manner may lead such readers into a series of wrong routes (you will find evidence of this in chapter 8). The reader in chapter 8 compre-hends this text very little and consequently does not read effectively. Lunzer and Gardner found that this was occurring far too often in secondary schools.

Activity 5

Look at the three texts opposite. Which do you think you would read rejectively? Which would you read receptively? And which reflectively?

Pronoun concord
The relation between the reflexive pronoun object and its subject may be seen as a special case of the concord between a pronoun and its antecedent, ie *the noun phrase for which it may be regarded as a substitute (see further 10.43). This type of concord may extend beyond clause boundaries. Thus the relative pronouns* who, whom *and* which *agree with their antecedent in the superordinate clause in gender, the first two being personal, and the last non-personal (4.117* ff)*:*

> The bag which I saw . . .   *[33]*
> The man who(m) I saw . . .   *[34]*

Whose *can be used with either animate or inanimate antecedents:*

> The house whose rafters were burnt . . .   *[35]*
> The man whose purse he stole . . .   *[36]*

There is a feeling, however, that whose *is more appropriate to personal antecedents, and some speakers cannot use an expression such as [35] without some feeling of uneasiness.*

(Quirk, Greenbaum, Leech, and Svartvik, 1972)

What is Open Learning?

Opening New Learning Opportunities

There is no universally agreed definition of Open learning. The essential idea, however, is that of opening up *new opportunities* for people to learn. Different Open learning schemes may do this in different ways – e.g. by dropping all entry requirements; by enabling Learners to study what they like, when and where they find most convenient, using whatever teaching media best suit them, and at their own individual pace; by providing special tutorial help; by allowing Learners to decide their own learning objectives and how (if at all) they are to be assessed.

(Manpower Services Commission (MSC), 1988)

He put down his grip and gazed about him. Saw the long, scrubbed table, the motley variety of chairs, the pine dresser laden with painted pottery plates and jugs and bowls. Copper saucepans, beautifully arranged by size, hung from a beam over the stove along with bunches of herbs and dried garden flowers. There was a basket, chair, ash white refrigerator, and a deep white china sink beneath the window, so that any person impelled to do the washing-up

could amuse himself at the same time by watching people's feet go by on the pavement.
(Pilcher, 1987)

From my experience it seems that children learn to read primarily on texts which they can read receptively. They then try to read in a similar fashion on the texts that require reflective reading. However, because of their poor reading habits, they end up reading rejectively. The children are often pretending to read, they are mimicking the serious reader but, because they are only imitating, they do not get the same results as the effective reader. Consequently they often fail to learn from the text.

Another quite different reading strategy is that used in proof-reading. This is where the reader is looking for errors in the text, the sort of errors that are made by the typist or writer. Proof-readers have to make themselves ignore the meaning of the text and concentrate on the type, because if one reads for meaning the printing errors are sometimes missed. Yet another type of reading is when the reader is looking to find a flaw in the writer's argument.

Another type of text that should alter the reader's strategy is the instructional text. If the text involves a sequence of actions such as a recipe or a science experiment, then the reader will have to read a section, do the activity, and then return to the text again. Young children are not used to this type of reading.

The significant point here is that reading is not one process, it is a collection of approaches. Pupils must be able to adapt to the demands of different reading situations. We should be teaching our youngsters how to become flexible in their reading. Most importantly we should teach children at the earliest opportunity that there are some major differences between expository and narrative texts. It must be stressed that these skills can be taught from the initial stages of learning to read and, from my experience, children who do learn them in the early part of their primary schooling learn to use them far more quickly and effectively than those who are not taught till later in their schooling.

In the words of Gagg (1968):

> . . . we need to remember that there are different levels of meaning-difficulty. A simple narrative story is no strain on a child beyond the recognition of the words. But a book which conveys a succession of facts – however interesting they are – calls for considerable thought over and above the physical reading process.
> (J. C. Gagg, © Times Newspapers Ltd, 1968)

Additionally Lavender (1983) suggests that flexible reading must be encouraged on informative books. Children must adapt to the demands.

> Although children should learn to roam across all kinds of books, nevertheless they still need to discover that the ones for information have many purposes. Some are browsers, some are starters, some aim to give a general survey of an area of human knowledge, some are for quick reference, some are biographies, some are in-depth of a particular topic, some are practical guides, some are documentaries, others seek to provide experience rather than overtly laying out a body of knowledge . . .
> (Lavender, 1983)

In the United States, suggestions are being made that children should be taught how to adapt from narrative to expository. For example, Anderson, Armbruster and Kantor (1980) concluded:

> We think the process required to read and understand expository text are different enough from those required to read narrative text that special training and practice is required before most students can be proficient at reading expository text.
> (Anderson, Armbruster and Kantor, 1980)

THE PRESENT STATE OF AFFAIRS IN OUR SCHOOLS AND THE DEMANDS OF THE NATIONAL CURRICULUM

Reports in the United Kingdom both recent and more dated have all suggested that teachers are not teaching children to become flexible readers. The Bullock Report (DES, 1975) stressed that children are not taught to develop their reading past the initial stages. More recent reports suggest that little has changed.

> The teaching of reading virtually ceases once the children can read aloud with reasonable accuracy at a reasonable speed. Yet to discontinue instruction at this point is rather like halting the training of a pianist once he can play the scales and a few elementary tunes.
> (Committee of Inquiry into Reading/DES, 1975)

The report of HMI (1989) on reading policy and practice in the period immediately preceding the introduction of the National Curriculum, has reported that:

> Although most year 6 pupils could cope with the informational handling aspects of reading such as using a contents page or an index, many had difficulty in retrieving and organising information for specific purposes. The threefold process of formulating appropriate questions, selecting and reading texts to find information and writing it up in their own words had not been taught to or acquired by many pupils.
> (DES, 1989)

However, the inspectors did find that:

> Schools saw it as an important obligation to help pupils master the complexities of advanced reading, but while they saw it as their duty, few gave coherent accounts of what these skills were and how they were to be developed.
> (DES, 1989)

In one school they found that children were floundering with even the simplest research tasks. They also claim that, in all the schools they visited, the younger children were not stretched sufficiently. Furthermore, few of the older pupils were helped to develop more sophisticated skills such as scanning or collating material from different sources.

> In short, advanced reading skills played too small a part in schools' planned provision for reading development.
> (DES, 1989)

The 1990s are seeing the implementation, in stages, of the National Curriculum. The National Curriculum for English is statutory for 5–11 year-olds at the time of writing. In the Cox committee's first report (DES, 1988) it is interesting to note that the attainment targets were to include 30% of all reading time to be spent on informational texts. In the interim report and the statutory orders this percentage has been omitted. I believe that this is a backward step: the committee obviously appreciated the importance of this type of reading, and the percentage demands of the statutory papers would have given informational reading a firm basis in all areas of the curriculum. Additionally, it would have created pressure to improve the quality of books published for children. Tann and Beard (1989) speculate that the reason for the committee's change of mind and its omission of specific percentages was that the original consultative paper had caused consternation amongst primary teachers 'because they did not know how to implement this amount of informational reading in their classrooms'. Nevertheless, this type of reading still holds a very important place in the National Curriculum. The Attainment Targets for Key Stage One include informative reading.

The Attainment Targets at level 2 demand that teachers should:

> in the course of topic or humanities work, ask the children to decide what they need to find out more about

and

> ask the children to find or suggest a book that might supply the information.

To reach level 3, children have to:

> think of at least three things to find out about the topic; suggest at least one book where such information might be found.

Further details of the demands of the National Curriculum in relation to informative reading will be explored on pages 77–8. However, it is pertinent to point out here that one of the demands of the attainment targets is that children understand what they read and do not simply copy verbatim from their books. For instance, the attainment target for level 3 (7 year-olds) is that pupils should be able to:

> Devise a clear set of questions that will enable them to select and use appropriate information sources and reference books from the class and school library.

This is a very demanding skill, and a very important one, but it has not been adequately taught in primary schools. Chapter 8 tries to help remedy this situation by suggesting strategies that enable children to read to learn and make notes in various forms. It appears that British children are currently no better at making notes than they are at effective reading. Lunzer and Gardner, (1979) found that most of what was supposed to be notemaking was in fact copying. Furthermore, it was in the area of topic work that they were most critical of the children's notemaking ability.

> . . . we have observed pupils engaged in topic work who treat their reading in a way that suggests that their main objective is to transfer the words of an author into their own books or file.
> (Lunzer and Gardner, 1979)

Other criticisms of British children's notemaking abilities will be pursued in chapter 8.

To sum up this section, I reiterate that young readers should have a variety of reading strategies readily available and that they should know which books demand committed reading, which are to be used for reference purposes, and which are for browsing. The crux of the matter is that young children should have a flexible approach to the reading task and this can only come about if they have been taught how to do this.

THE IMPORTANCE OF INFORMATIVE READING

Activity 6

What sort of reading do you do at home?

You probably found that as well as reading narratives for pleasure, you read the following items: timetables, messages, newspapers, notes, letters from friends, formal letters, recipes, shopping lists, notices, advertisements, bills.

Many of the reading activities are for finding out. It seems to be that one of the life skills that we should be encouraging children to acquire is that of reading for information, because, unless they can do this in today's literature-dependent society, they may find it difficult to cope.

Activity 7

What sort of reading do you do at work?

In the workplace, the majority of jobs require employees to be able to read informative material rather than narrative. You will probably be surprised how little narrative reading is required in the typical workplace. The jobs with higher salaries usually demand even more informative reading.

It is also true that informational reading is used more and more the further up the educational ladder the reader goes. It often seems to me that we have our priorities wrong in this country. It is informative reading and writing that should be emphasised in our schools, and not the reverse.

This book is based on the principle that reading for meaning must be taught from the beginning. There is very little point teaching children to read by rote, with no understanding. The understanding must go hand in hand with the deciphering of words. The basic requirements are to understand and make meaning from a text, not necessarily word-fluency. It is therefore important to consider how children are taught to read in this country. It will be remembered that most children in this country learn to read on narrative texts.

HOW DO CHILDREN LEARN TO READ?

In Britain, not all children are taught reading by the same method. A number of approaches are used, and often appear equally successful in their initial results. In other words, the children are able to say the words out loud, and they score reasonably well on reading tests. Unfortunately, a child's comprehension does not necessarily tally with his or her ability to read aloud; a fluent oral reader may have poor recall, and a stumbling reader may understand what he or she has read.

There are two views on reading which underlie all methods and approaches. The two contrasting theoretical perspectives are called 'Top-down' and 'Bottom-up'. All methods of teaching reading can be said to emphasise one of these views rather than the other. The Bottom-up theory is basically the 'breaking the code' method. This approach was used in schools in the early half of this century and includes the Phonic, Alphabetic, and Whole Word methods. The theory suggests that we must know the parts before attacking the whole. The Top-down theory of reading takes the opposite approach, with the belief that one must seek the whole text as means of gaining a message. The reader starts with a number of assumptions or hypotheses about the text and then slowly, through the process of reading, either accepts or rejects these. The psycholinguistic approaches come under this category.

The old controversy over which methods work best has been raised again recently in the popular press. The crucial question though, is 'Are we equipping our youngsters with skills that they will find useful in today's heavily literate society?'. In other words 'Can they find out?'. I would like to suggest further that the recent research on text analysis has begun to alter the emphasis in reading, although a number of schools are not yet conversant with this evidence.

Until relatively recently, materials to help readers have concentrated on the sentence and units smaller than this structure. It was assumed that a text was just a succession of separate sentences, thematically related. It was not thought necessary to deal with the structure of the whole text. However Grellet has stated:

> If reading is to be efficient, the structure of longer units such as the paragraph or the whole text must be understood. It is no good studying a text as though it were a series of independent units.
> (Grellet, 1981)

I have included in chapter 8 a piece of work that illustrates this very point. The child was reading sentence-by-sentence and was unable to see the text as a whole. The child was probably taught to read by being asked to read just one page of a book at a time. The modern approach is to encourage the child to read a meaningful chunk – either the whole book or enough 'to get into' the story.

It was suggested earlier that the teaching of reading can take many forms and that one of the problems of teaching children to comprehend is that some educationalists believe that reading should be taught in stages. Some teachers may take the approach that the 'basics' of reading should be taught first and that only later can the children develop their reading. I cannot support this view for it often impedes the teaching of reading. Children taught using this approach get into bad habits and believe that reading does not involve extracting meaning. This view of reading is epitomised by the following quote from Kilpatrick, McCall and Palmer.

> By the middle years (ten to thirteen) most pupils have mastered the basic mechanics of reading. They have learnt to read and are ready to start reading to learn.
> (Kilpatrick, McCall and Palmer, 1982)

This suggests that, until the age of 10, children are not reading for meaning at all but are merely voicing the words. I support the contrasting view of Whysall (1987) who believes that reading for learning must be taught right from the beginning.

> We should be teaching book and text handling skills in some form from the earliest stages of the child's reading development.
> (Whysall, 1987)

He continues:

> We should dispense with the idea that the teaching of an interrogative style of reading begins only after a child has received a lot of experience of passive story type reading . . . we attempt to wrest children away from a set of reading habits we have spent perhaps years cultivating,
> (Whysall, 1987)

Whysall believes, and I wholeheartedly agree, that children must be taught how to cope with informative texts in a real situation. The most effective way of teaching young children how to learn from texts is in the process of undertaking a project. Past attempts to teach reading for information in isolation, away from the rest of the curriculum, have been dismissed as ineffectual. It has been found that there is no transfer of work on specific aspects of reading if it is not integrated into the whole reading curriculum. My work and the work of many others support this (Lunzer and Gardner, 1979; Cole and Gardner, 1981; Bulman, 1985; Avon Schools, 1986; Nisbet and Shucksmith, 1986).

Many colleges and universities set up study skills courses in the seventies and early eighties to try to teach their first year students more effective reading and notemaking strategies but the evidence is that the students failed to change their habits even though they were able to perform correctly in the special classes (Pugh, 1978). Nisbet and Shucksmith (1986) suggest that the help had come too late in the students' education, and that reading habits had already became too established. Bulman (1985) refers to children of primary age and claims that:

> children are often taught a variety of skills during their last two years in primary school, including how to use a reference book index, how to skim read, how to write reports and so on. However, if these same . . . trained children were let loose on project work, the chances are that these skills would fly out of the window as they set to copying, pasting, and keeping very busy with whatever aspect of the topic took their fancy.
> (Bulman, 1985)

It must now be commonly accepted, as Irving and Snape (1978) have stressed, that the time to teach these reference skills is in the infant school as well as further up the educational ladder. This is further supported by an Avon schools report:

> We do not think these skills are acquired in isolation. They cannot be taught at any one stage and retained for later use without being constantly reinforced.
> (Issues 3 – Can a Kangaroo Jump?, 1986)

In the past, some children have been taught how to use reference books, but they have usually been taught in circumstances divorced from the relevant work situations. Project work is the natural place for teaching children how to use expository texts as it requires them to use their reference skills in an immediate and real situation.

PROJECT WORK

Children's investigative work is not a recent phenomenon on the British educational scene. It was first suggested in the Dalton Plan and the idea was pursued in the Hadow Report in 1931. Since then, projects, topics and themes have increasingly found favour in a large number of schools. They became most popular and truly recognised after the publication of the Plowden Report (1967) which recommended the notions of activity-based, investigative, autonomous learning. Since the golden days of popularity though, the inadequacies of the present system of investigative work have become apparent. However, good project work is still, as Sarah Tann points out,

> the epitome of all that is best in British primary schools.
> (Tann, 1988)

Three different names can be used for investigative work. These are 'projects', 'topics' and 'thematic work'. They did originally have definitions, but over the years the differences have been eroded and the terms have all come to mean any type of investigative, non-subject based work. The three terms are often used interchangeably in schools, and so the same will be done in this book.

Project work has become so popular in England and Wales that most children will nowadays experience some form of project work in their years of schooling. One of the problems of project work, however, is that the approach taken can vary so widely. In fact, although project work is still highly favoured, it has collected many criticisms over the years.

One of the most damaging condemnations of the project approach was by the Black Papers (Cox and Dyson, 1971; Cox and Boyson, 1977). These contained a sweeping criticism of what was supposed to be the wild progressive movement. The authors referred to projects as 'a rag-bag curriculum', because many schools did not have any sort of policy on projects. Little thought had been devoted in most schools to what they expected the children to be able to learn from the approach. Teachers assumed that content was all that mattered.

A second major criticism of project work is that children copy verbatim from the information books provided rather than read to learn. As was discussed earlier, the Bullock Report (Committee of Inquiry into Reading/DES, 1975) found that much of the writing done in the name of topic work amounted to no more than copying. The two HMI reports of 1978 and 1989 found a similar picture. I have found during my work in schools that teachers know that their children often resort to copying. However, the same teachers admitted that they knew few strategies to help their pupils break this habit.

The third major criticism of project work is suggested by the studies of Ann Irving (1982), David Wray (1985), and Sarah Tann (1987): that in schools there is a tendency to emphasise content at the expense of skills. One of the reasons why teachers did not teach these skills seemed to be that they did not really know which skills were involved in project work. Most teachers had never been trained in how to carry out investigation work in the classroom (Wray, 1985). Again, this is supported by my own question-naire of London teachers.

The most recent research on project skills suggests that one basic difficulty is the fact that the process of finding out appears to be common sense to most educated people. Many of the skills are therefore second nature and instinctive to teachers. Martin and Buck (1984) worked on trying to improve project work in the classroom before realising that:

> The skills we were observing and rating, the skills we expected the children to demonstrate, had never been specified in our meetings, let alone specifically taught.
> (Martin and Buck, 1984)

It must be remembered here that a significant finding was reported earlier, namely that it is the experience of higher educational establish-ments that when research skills are taught at this level the teaching is often unsuccessful. However, because projects involve finding out by experi-mentation, exploration or research, they provide the opportunity for the introduction of study techniques that enable children to learn how to learn. Wray (1985), Marland (1982), Nisbet and Shucksmith (1986) all see information skills as central to the development of children's learning because it is only when people know how to learn that they can go on learning. We are living through an information explosion, so the adults of tomorrow will need to be able to find out rather than be expected to have the facts at their fingertips.

Additionally, even though we have a National Curriculum based on subject areas, the government guidelines and advice from professional bodies suggests that work in schools should still be project based. I quote from a report written collectively by a number of professional associations working together:

> all the (government) documents we looked at emphasise the im-portance of organising contexts for children's learning that cross subject boundaries.
> (Association for Science Education, 1989)

I think teachers who have been used to using the project method will continue to use it, because there is no doubt that children's motivation is greatly increased during project work. The important point is that teachers must use it to advantage and must therefore know how to teach children to read for information.

CONCLUSION

This chapter has discussed in brief terms how children learn to read and how there are two schools of thought on whether children should be taught reading to learn from the initial stages. Various reading strategies were discussed and it was suggested that it is important for young children to acquire these flexible reading habits from an early age.

2 Books for pleasure or for information

It must be stressed, from the outset, that children are not necessarily proficient readers. It takes time for children to become proficient or effective readers. It is thought by some (Pugh, 1978) that it is not until children are about 13 years-old that they find reading as informative as listening. Bereiter (1985) suggests that in many kinds of casual reading a superficial level of comprehension may suffice, but that high school students are often unable to read more complex texts because they do not have the necessary 'higher powered strategies'.

DIFFERENCES BETWEEN ORAL AND WRITTEN LANGUAGE

The findings of Lunzer and Gardner (1979) suggest that children are unable, without tutoring, to take advantage of the permanence of text. In texts there are no intonations, stresses or rhythms to help the reader along as there are in oral language. For example in spoken language, vocal stresses can give clues that the speaker is changing track and is starting to talk about a new topic. Another problem with texts is that readers have to work out for themselves which words belong to which phrase, whereas in spoken language this is easier. Written and spoken language differ in certain linguistic aspects too. For instance, Perera (1984) points out that written language uses different grammatical constructions and discourse structures.

Texts are self-sufficient and largely independent of any physical context. For instance, suppose in a spoken conversation, someone says 'That Mercedes needs a new exhaust' when a car is making a lot of noise. A listener who does not know the vocabulary can guess the meaning of 'Mercedes' and quite a lot about the meaning of the word 'exhaust' from the situation. Texts do not have these contextual clues: the author has to write about the situation using specific language. If a reader does not understand a written text, the author cannot reword the facts or concepts. There is no feedback from reader to author. The author has to aim at a group audience and within that group there will be a great variety of backgrounds. Some readers might find the text easy whilst others find it impossible to understand. Home background may have an influence too.

DIFFERENCES BETWEEN NARRATIVE AND EXPOSITORY TEXTS

I now turn to the more specific area of expository material found mainly in secondary schools, this discussion is followed by an analysis of how these factors affect the primary aged child.

A useful definition of expository text is that provided by Tonjes:

> Expository text is that which seeks to explain.
> (Tonjes, 1986)

Rose Macaulay was perhaps one of the first people to write on the simplicity of narration compared to expository text.

> Many persons read and like fiction. It does not tax the intelligence and the intelligence of most of us can so ill afford taxation, that we rightly welcome any reading matter which avoids this.
> (Macaulay, 1885–1956, in *Expository Material*, by Otto and White)

Teachers are still endeavouring to point out the differences to children and it has taken over a century for educationalists to realise the demands of the expository text. As Perera notes:

> The structures of fiction are familiar to children while the more varied structures of non-fiction are not.
> (Perera, 1986b)

The Books in Schools Survey concluded that in our schools there is more emphasis on fiction than on expository texts.

> Primary schools promote the narrative at the expense of the non-narrative.
> (Davies, 1986)

Whitehead (1977) and Heather (1984) found that children do read expository texts but that they tend to do so only in the pursuit of hobbies, or in their areas of expertise.

We have to recognise that the differences between expository texts and fiction are not usually taught in schools, and that children have to pick up the requirements of the different registers by their own devices. As Calfee and Curley have claimed:

The gap between the primer level and the reading demands of 'real life' is substantial. . . . We believe that many youngsters fail to make the step from the primer to the textbook.
(Calfee and Curley, 1984)

There are a surprisingly large number of differences between narrative and expository texts.

Activity 1

Make a list of the differences and similarities between narrative and expository texts. Once you have done this, compare your list with the table below.

A COMPARISON OF NARRATIVE AND EXPOSITORY TEXTS

Narrative	Expository
General	
The intention is to entertain	The intention is to describe, explain or comment upon
Stories are told/read to children from an early age	Children hear less expository texts read out loud
Narrative texts are based on themes, topics or experiences with which children are likely to be familiar	By their very nature, expository texts inform their readers about something with which they are less familiar
It tells a story	There is no story
The format is familiar	The format is very varied and is less likely to be familiar
Schools promote reading of narrative text	Schools are less likely to promote expository reading
The emphasis is on enjoyment	The emphasis is on learning
Children learn to read on narrative	Children often do not experience expository text in early readers
There is only one reading strategy to be learnt	Flexible reading strategies should be used
Narrative is read from beginning to end	Expository text should enable the reader to select parts to read. It could often be read in any order
Fantasy and make believe are used	Expository text is factual
There is less material to absorb	There is much material to absorb

Narrative	Expository
Structure	
Narratives can be varied but they conform to a story grammar – they have a beginning, a happening and an end	No story grammar. No accepted or recognised pattern
The story is designed to keep pulling the reader along	The text may be interesting but will not have cliff-hangers and climaxes throughout
The text may be broken into chapters	The text is broken into headings and sub-headings
Layout	
Dust jacket likely to show one scene from the plot	Dust jacket may indicate the whole field of topic
The blurb on the back cover sets the scene and a little of the story is given away	The blurb on the reverse expands upon the title
Illustrations aim to help the reader identify with the characters or place. They add to the story	Illustrations – the reader is expected to learn from the illustrations. They are more likely to be photographs, diagrams, maps or charts
Captions are rare in story books	Captions are often used: one for each illustration. Captions can help the reader to select which parts of the text to read
Introductions are unusual in children's novels	Introduction – a good introduction tells the reader what they will read about, what to watch out for and what they will learn
Headings other than chapter headings are not found in narrative	Headings are used to break down units of text into smaller sections to enable the reader to select parts to read
Index – not found in narrative	Index – only found in expository text
Contents – the function of which is to entice the reader but not to give away the contents of each chapter	Contents – the function of the contents list is to give as many clues as possible as to the contents of each chapter
Bibliography – not usually found	The books referred to by the author should be listed in a bibliography. Often, a list of further books to study is also provided
Glossaries rarely included	Glossaries are a dictionary of useful or 'stopper' words

Narrative	Expository
Page numbers are not of any real importance except to keep one's place	Page numbers are often very necessary so that the reader can read selectively

Language

Narrative	Expository
The language is often elaborate, descriptive, and similar to spoken language	The language is often terse and concise
The language is familiar, e.g. direct speech	The language often uses specialised technical terms: it may demand prior knowledge, include unfamiliar concepts, and have supplementary material to the main thread of text
The past tense is used more frequently than the present tense	Present tense is often used
Little use of the verb 'to be'	Frequent use of the verb 'to be'
More use of action verbs, stating actions or happenings	More use of relational verbs
Frequent use of 'I'	Little use of 'I'
High use of pronouns, especially 'he' and 'she'	Fewer pronouns, with more use of 'it' and 'they'
	Frequent use of phases such as 'there are many kinds of'
	Frequent use of familiar words in a technical context e.g. 'family', 'bed'
Fewer words between subject and verb	More words between subject and verb
Connectives tend to be more familiar and easier to understand e.g. 'and', 'but'.	Connectives tend to be less familiar and more difficult to understand e.g. 'consequently', 'however'.

Narrative texts need not be stories or novels: they can be personal experiences, legends, parables, reports of events, fairy stories, fables, classics or romances. The important notion is that they all have their own widely recognised structure. Much research has been carried out on narrative texts and it has been found that they follow a standard sequence, which has come to be known as 'story grammar'. Much research has been focused on the importance of story grammar to understanding. Kintsch and van Dijk (1978) and others indicate that in all narrative texts there is a series of events. These happenings do not go smoothly and there is always a complication or problem. A typical story commences with 'orientation' which gives the temporal and spatial setting for the story. This sets the scene for the events which follow. Next the problem (sometimes called the complication), occurs and this is then resolved. This is called 'resolution'. The problem might or might not be successfully resolved. At the end there may be a section which gives the reason for the story: this is called a coda.

Much less research has been carried out on expository texts. Bereiter (1978) was surprised when he realised that discourse analysis was overwhelmingly concerned with narrative. However, Christie (1984) has contributed a body of work on expository registers and she concludes that expository texts are:

> Those in which the intention is to describe, explain, or comment upon some matter or offer factual accounts or descriptions.
> (Christie, 1984)

Kress (1982) points out that expository texts have no beginning, no end, and no climax. They are often written in the present tense whereas narrative is often written in the past tense and he suggests that the factual sentences often use the verb 'to be'. Similarly, Christie believes that narrative texts have more action verbs stating actions or happenings e.g. 'came' while expository texts have a high proportion of relational verbs such as 'are' as in the phrase 'there are many types of . . .'. So we must conclude that the structures of the two types of text are quite different.

Several studies such as Baker (1978) and McClure, Mason and Barnitz (1979) provide evidence that sequentially ordered texts are generally easier to read. Narrative texts are more likely to have a chronological order and are therefore easier to understand. Information books have no sequential story to keep the reader going, and may often be read in any chapter order. In fiction, the read often becomes easier once the reader has got to grips with the character and storyline, but non-fiction is equally difficult all the way through.

Kintsch (1982) carried out much work on expository texts and suggests that, to comprehend an expository text the reader must first have a general knowledge of the subject area and second the knowledge and abilities to apply the correct reading strategies to these expository texts. Christie (1984) makes the obvious but very vital point that while expository texts may be shown to differ from each other, they are all markedly different from narrative genres. It will be shown in later chapters that there is an enormous variety of registers in children's books.

LINGUISTIC FEATURES

Katharine Perera (1986a) looked at the special difficulty of the language of non-fiction books. She made detailed linguistic comparisons and as a result of this work and of her other studies of texts, she concluded that the problems children encounter with factual texts come under four language categories: vocabulary, linguistic features, register and grammar.

Vocabulary

In non-fiction books, Perera points out, the text often uses a technical vocabulary. Another problem is that the words used often have at least two meanings, one a familiar interpretation and the second a specialised meaning. When young pupils read these words they often become confused: for example, the word 'caravan' which, in familiar usage, means a house on wheels also has the unfamiliar meaning of a company of travellers. 'Bed' is another word that has two common meanings but, to children, the meaning associated with sleeping is more likely to come to mind than the meaning to do with flowers. 'Present' 'family' and 'relief' are other words with two meanings which children often confuse. Hull (1976) also found that children were confused by these types of words. Further evidence of this confusion is given in Chapter 8.

Perera found that there is a difficult dividing line between the use of technical words and the use of jargon in expository texts. Firstly, there is the essential specialist technical vocabulary – the language of the subject or what Halliday (1973, 1975) calls the topic of discourse – those words that express precisely the terms and concepts of that subject. Secondly, there is the specialist use of non-technical words such as 'settlement' which have more than one meaning. But to compound the difficulties encountered there is also 'textbook vocabulary'. These are words or phrases that are not part of the pupils' language, and are of no use to them outside the school environment, but which are non-subject specific. As Mobley (1987) claims, these are the words that should have no place in textbooks, because they only serve to increase the remoteness and the mystification of school learning. Textbook vocabulary includes phrases and words such as 'let us assume', 'in truth', 'accordingly', 'in direct proportion to', 'thereupon', 'correlation', 'attribution', 'whence', 'on that account'.

Another problem Perera identified is the fact that children have to learn to recognise synonyms. She gives the following pair of sentences as an example:
'The general ordered his troops to fight well. Caesar was always in a foul mood.'

Children have to understand that Caesar and the general are the same person if they are to understand this text.

Linguistic features

Perera found differences between the two sorts of texts in the amount of direct speech used. There was no direct speech in the non-fiction, but there was some direct speech in nearly half of the fictional texts that she analysed. Perera believes that this direct speech probably makes the text nearer to that of oral everyday speech, and therefore easier to understand. Another interesting finding was that there were far fewer pronouns in the non-fiction than the fiction, and there was also a contrast in the type of pronoun used. Half of the non-fiction pronouns were the impersonal 'it' and 'they' while 84% of the fiction pronouns referred to people. All of these differences add to the remoteness of expository text.

Grammar

Perera suggested that the sentence patterns found in expository texts are not very often used in speech. First, there were on average more than twice as many words between subject and verb in non-fiction as in fiction, and there were differences in the verb phrases and the noun phrases between the two groups of books.

In her 1984 work Perera also found that fiction books had more connectives than non-fiction. Connectives are those words that connect one sentence (or part of a sentence) with another such as 'and', 'then', 'nevertheless'. However, she claims that these connectives are probably more important in non-fictional writing, because they give the reader clues to the organisation of the text. Words such as 'similarly', and 'however', carry a great deal of weight in non-fiction. In my own small study similar results were discovered by comparing twenty fiction and non-fictional books I found that there were 50% more connectives in the fictional books than the factual books, and that the type of connective used was different.

Rogers (1974) found that a great range of connectives is used in children's books. He found 128 different connectives being used, some of which might be familiar to secondary children but many of which are very difficult to comprehend such as 'thus', 'nevertheless', 'therefore', 'similarly', 'consequently', 'hence', 'instead' and 'moreover'. The structural signposts such as 'first' or 'one reason' are more common in non-fictional texts and are also of more importance to the reader.

It is suggested in these studies that connectives are very useful to the reader and that it is the lack of connectives in non-fictional texts that actually makes the texts harder. Anderson, Armbruster and Kantor (1980) in a comprehensive piece of work suggested that, when texts are written with short sentences, the meaning link goes, and hence the reader has the additional problem of inference to cope with. They stressed that books lacking connectives and books written to satisfy readability formulae actually have increased concept densities. In the same way Herber (1970) recognised the importance of connectives:

> Students can use the signal words to establish mind sets as they read, enabling them to follow the author better through the development of the topic.
> (Herber, 1970)

Pearson (1982) found that sentences such as 'The peasants revolted because the king raised taxes.' with the connective 'because' were easier to interpret than 'The king raised taxes. The peasants revolted.'. In a later study he asked some 9 year-olds about connectives. He asked the children to read some sentences with no connectives and some sentences with simple connectives. The children preferred to work with the sentences that had connectives.

From other bodies of research we know that for a written text to be successful it is necessary for there to be links between sentences. However, such links alone are not sufficient for meaning to be obtained. It is possible to make up pseudo-discourses in which each sentence is linked impeccably to the preceding one, and yet the result is a lack of global coherence. Writers have to impose an overall pattern of organisation on their work, as well as taking care of local connections between sentences.

> There is an unfortunate tendency for writers of non-fiction books for the youngest readers to produce discourses that are really just collections of unconnected sentences on a single topic. This style of composition is even reflected in the layout, which frequently gives a new line to each sentence.
> (Perera, 1986a)

Anderson and Armbruster (1981) suggest that it is because children have less experience of reading that connectives are, in fact, more important to them. Adults have more experience of reading and they use this to go back over a text and try to work out exactly what the relationships are in the text.

The importance of this discussion on connectives will become evident in Chapters 3 and 4: many children's information books have limited their use of connectives because the authors or editors mistakenly think this makes the text easier to read.

TEXTBOOKS AND INFORMATION BOOKS

Reports suggest that textbooks are still the mainstay of the secondary school even if they are not used as much as they were in the past.

> Almost without exception, the textbook is still seen as the staple diet in the classroom; it is regarded as an essential, indeed the main, teaching aid . . . teachers are able, in every case, to make cogent and convincing arguments in support of the central role of the textbook.
> (Ingham and Brown, 1986)

The use of textbooks may still be common practice in schools, but their place has been subject to widespread and continuing criticism since the sixties. To return to evidence from Lunzer and Gardner (1979) the data shows that the effectiveness of a textbook as a means of learning is minimal. In fact Lunzer and Gardner went so far as to suggest that secondary texts may well be the cause of the 'retreat from print' which has been found to occur in young teenagers. They found that most of the books that the children were expected to use were, by the results of readability analysis, far too difficult for the intended age range. They claimed that children learned much less than they might from the texts because the texts were presenting difficulties not just in terms of conceptual content, but because of the way in which they were written (Lunzer and Gardner, 1979). In fact, the findings were so gloomy that Lunzer and Gardner concluded that reading for learning in the secondary school was an enormous problem.

Anderson, Armbruster and Kantor (1980) found that in the USA there were similar problems with reading to learn. They suggested that in the States:

> Teachers in elementary grades do not use textbooks as a primary learning vehicle.
> (Anderson, Armbruster and Kantor, 1980)

They believe that it is the quality of the textbooks that actually stop the teachers from using them.

In the sixties teachers were beginning to realise that children could not cope with the books in the secondary school, and this led to a period during which simplified worksheets were commonplace. Teachers often misunderstood readability factors and believed that if they wrote their own 'textbooks' according to readability factors, children would be able to cope with the data better. But the use of worksheets has generally not been a success, and as Ingham and Brown suggest, worksheets can be positively harmful.

> One suspects that many pupils, continually faced with seeking out a single word or piece of information from a short worksheet, will eventually become too lazy, or even afraid to use a textbook.
> (Ingham and Brown, 1986)

Teachers have tried to do away with textbooks altogether in some situations as Wishart (1986) sums up:

> At present much of the pupil's success is in fact the teachers' success in circumnavigating the difficulties of textbooks by offering their own explanation.
> (Wishart, 1986)

One of the reasons that children find textbooks difficult, Torbe and Medway (1981) claim, is because of their register. Chapman and Louw (1986), in a study on the registers of secondary school books, concluded that there is a reading register clash in the early secondary school. They believe that this clash is not completely resolved until the pupils reach the level of tertiary education. I will pursue this subject in Chapters 5 and 6.

One final point should be made concerning textbooks: as will be seen in later chapters, they are clearly not up to the standard of adult expository texts. Bloom (1985) sums the situation up well:

> Textbooks do not often contain the balance between main idea and details that other reference books have. Most books make a statement, reformulate it in a different way and pad out round it to make the information clear and digestible. In most textbooks each short paragraph is made up of sentences/statements which are really a paragraph in themselves. The information is thus very dense and makes for difficult reading.
> (Bloom 1985)

Primary information books

Up to this point I have discussed mainly texts designed for secondary children. However, the emphasis needs now to be put on books specifically found in Primary Schools. Detailed analysis will be made in later chapters.

First, a factor of emphasis needs to be pointed out which may not be immediately obvious. In surveys of how children used books in the primary and the secondary school, Beverton (1986) and Lunzer and Gardner (1979) found that there were well defined differences between the ways in which books were used in the two different types of school. Fiction is read in primary schools by individuals or small groups in the classroom, whereas in secondary schools individual reading is usually carried out in the library. However, in the classroom they read class readers. By contrast, non-fiction texts on a variety of topics are used in the primary school individually, but in the secondary schools they are used as class readers i.e. textbooks. So in the two types of schools there were opposite situations. Beverton (1986) also found that in the last term at primary school 116 children read (or at least used) 155 fiction books while they used only 80 non-fiction books. In the first term at the secondary level they read only 46 fiction and 62 non-fiction books, so the balance had changed quite dramatically. It seems from Beverton's work that the children are inadequately prepared for this change of reading diet.

The term 'information' books in this text refers to all those books that are used for finding out purposes. In a primary school, these books might be from the school library, or they might be books borrowed from other libraries as part of a 'project loan'. The term non-fiction has deliberately not been used. The term 'information books' is not used for encyclopaedias, dictionaries and other reference books, many of which are not designed for school purposes.

The two authoritative works on children's information books in this country are by Peggy Heeks (1981) and Margery Fisher (1972) but neither of these works is in the form of research, or of a rigorous nature. They are written more as reviews of information books, with some suggested useful titles for teachers.

Fisher's work concentrates on the instructive element of children's non-fiction books, and she describes books under a number of themes. Fisher is often critical of the books. For instance:

A child uses information books to assemble what he knows, what he feels, what he sees as well as to collect new facts . . . he needs books which combine warm individuality and clear exposition, a mingling of words that colour the subject and words that clarify it, a recognition of past as well as present. He seldom finds such books.
(Fisher, 1972)

Peggy Heeks is often critical of the language used in information books. She is especially critical of the use of adjectives such as 'wonderful' and 'marvellous' in Natural History texts. Heeks also claims that children's information books are far too dependent on the author's attitudes and do not often give a balanced view. She claims:

> An information book must communicate facts and ideas to its readers, of whatever age or capacity, in such a way that they will develop the will and mental equipment to assess these facts and ideas. In the broadest sense, an information book is a teacher, and the role of a teacher is to lead his pupils towards a considered independence of thought and action.
> (Heeks, 1981)

Much of the literature on children's books including the work of Fisher and Heeks claims that the presentation of books is improving but often to the detriment of the books as a whole.

> The topic books of today are smarter, better produced, more sophisticated than those of the past, but forty years ago, when writers seemed to have been less conscious of their attitude to the young, there was more room for style and individuality.
> (Fisher, 1972)

In a more recent but smaller piece of work, Mobley (1987) criticises the illustration of modern children's information books. She claims that the print on the page meanders through the drawings, especially in books written for the younger reader. This meandering is not only confusing, she says, but makes the print difficult to read, since there is often a reduction in legibility. Mobley observed also that the illustrations must be of high quality so that the pupils can be taught to 'read' them and gain information from them.

Mobley feels that children's information books should not be so well organised nor so well written that they 'promote uncritical and passive learning'. If all the thinking and sorting out has been done by the writer, she says:

> There is no need for the readers to be active interrogators of the text at all.
> (Mobley, 1987)

This opinion is perhaps valid in the case of adult books: to produce books that do not stretch adults can be seen, in the long term, as unhelpful. However, this cannot be true for primary children. They must be given good models so that they can learn how useful information books can be.

Shirley Paice (1984) carried out a small piece of research into books on honeybees. She found that the books were exceedingly poor and that the information in them was often inaccurate. She concluded that in the simplified books such as the Macdonald Starters, the language was so terse that in some cases it was actually wrong.

Margaret Meek (1982) also expressed dissatisfaction with the topic books which are found in every primary school. These books, she suggests, are in schools to represent learning rather than to promote it. She is of the opinion that each book should be written by an expert in the subject so that the topic comes alive. This assertion is controversial: there are two schools of thought as to who should write children's information books. One believes that they should be written by a subject specialist and the other believes that they should be written by authors who have a background in education and who write in a readable way.

Connected with the difficulty of writing information texts is the fact that the job of writing for young children is often given no status. It has been suggested in the past by both writers and reviewers that anybody can write for young children: this is clearly a fallacy.

The books available for children of infant age are just as weak. Heeks pointed out in 1981 that:

> Teachers and librarians still complain that publishers do not pay enough attention to the lower end of the age scale. The problem is not so much a lack of books as a lack of those showing an understanding of young children's limitations and teachers aims.
> (Heeks, 1981)

The article by Davies (1985) on introducing information skills to infants was also exceedingly scathing about many of the books currently found in infant school libraries.

When this problem was first voiced there was a spate of so-called easy books published (e.g. Macdonald Starters). Some of these were so successful that they were found in nearly every school (Heeks, 1981). Few if any information books aimed at the very young had been published before, and they became an immediate success story for the publishers (Heeks, 1982). But teachers in those early days had not looked closely enough at the content: the editors (these books tend to be written by editorial boards rather than by individual authors) were more concerned with sales figures than with the words in the texts. It will suffice here to quote from an American article by Anderson, Armbruster and Kantor:

> We are not sure why bright, dedicated people are not producing better quality text for children.
> (Anderson, Armbruster and Kantor, 1980)

Another problem which has not been voiced, but which might contribute to the poor quality of children's books, is the fact that many reviewers and publishers of children's information books do not know in sufficient detail how these books are actually being used in the classroom. Neither do they know what reading demands are made on the children by the teachers. Reviewers (and publishers) may actually perpetuate the problem because they are not reading experts.

Information books for children tend to be published in series. This is understandable because it keeps the cost of production and marketing down. The important point here is that publishers tend to try to sell their books as sets, and the unsuspecting teacher does not realise that the quality of the books in a series can vary considerably so that each title requires individual assessment. A worrying trend is the amount of structure that publishers impose on their authors. I have had numerous authors come to me complaining that they are unable to write as they wish, or to act on suggestions that I might make, because they are prevented from doing so by the publishers. The publishers argue that information books must sell in large numbers, therefore they must have books written to a format. This will enable the books to be printed for foreign audiences: it is questionable whether this really should be a priority in children's book publishing.

Publishers and teachers have agreed that the visual impact and presentation of books for children is very important. This is where it is generally agreed that books have moved forward a great deal. The problem is that although these books are now more attractive, it is no easier to extract information from them. The text is not necessarily improved. In fact during an interview that I held with a senior editor of one of the large publishing houses, the editor admitted to me that in his company no-one was too concerned about the text, as long as the book looked presentable.

CONCLUSION

This chapter concentrated on books: discussing first, books in general, then textbooks and finally narrowing down to information books for the primary age range. The work suggests that information books are not given much prominence in research and that studies that have been made have generally seen the books as weak.

3 Structure and organisation of children's information books

As part of my research I analysed three hundred children's project books. I went to one of the large urban local education authorities' libraries and borrowed books on ten different topics. The librarians selected the books for me, on the understanding that they were to be aimed at the junior age group of children (i.e. 7–11 year-olds). The project titles were Castles, Houses, Local Environment, Food, Romans, Water, Animals, Explorers, Rivers and Time. I looked at three aspects of the books: structure and organisation, readability and register. This chapter is devoted to the structure and organisation of the books, while Chapters 4 and 5 concentrate on their readability and register respectively.

STRUCTURAL GUIDERS

'Structural guiders' is a term that I have coined to cover the organisational and flagging devices used in books. This chapter starts by pointing out the usefulness of structural guiders in general to the effective reader. It then highlights the importance of each structural guider in turn. I give the results of my research and give details of how many books have each structural guider. I also look at the organisation of the books.

The importance of structural guiders

The National Curriculum for the teaching of English (1989) is demanding that children are able to use books to retrieve information without teacher support. This emphasis is reflected in the number of books that have been published recently on study skills. There are also many books published on the methodology of the teaching of reading: a number of these emphasise the essential nature of what are termed here structural guiders.

Much of the emphasis in study skills books has been on the importance of 'surveying', a technique which grew in stature with the popularity of the 'SQ3R' technique (see page 133). Surveying is a skill that allows the reader to assess a book very quickly. It involves looking at the dust jacket, skimming the blurb and assessing the book's relevance to one's specific needs.

Even when not using SQ3R techniques, though, children should be able to use the structural guiders in information books to advantage. Surveying, as Wray (1985) and many others have pointed out, is only one of the many skills involved in using information books that should be taught to primary aged children.

There seems to be a general consensus as to which parts of an information book are required to enable us to survey it, and there is agreement that all readers should develop the skill of using structural guiders. For instance, the Open University text (1976) strongly recommends that primary aged children, in order to become effective and efficient readers, should use the following features of a book:

> contents, layout and design, approach and difficulty level, date of publication, publisher's reputation, author's qualifications, foreword, preface, introduction, chapter headings and sub-headings, glossary, bibliography and references, list of illustrations.
> (Chapman and Hoffman, Open University, 1976)

Hounsell and Martin (1980) in their checklist of information skills mentioned a similar range of useful structural guiders. Nearly all methodology books (i.e. those books teaching study skills and reading techniques) agree upon the fundamental importance of structural guiders in books of a non-narrative nature. Bulman (1985) states:

> Many aspects of a book provide useful information on its contents before any real reading has been attempted. Title, author, publisher, date of publication, blurb, cover design, contents page, index, glossary and preface, all provide very valuable clues that the pupil should be able to recognise.
> (Bulman, 1985)

Hagberg (1975) and Cooke (1978) have suggested a similar list for younger readers.

In American publications the student readers and their teachers receive similar advice.

> Content area teachers will find that explaining the functions of prefaces, table of contents, indexes, appendices, glossaries, footnotes and bibliographies will be well worth the effort because of the increased efficiency with which the student will be able to use books.
> (Roe, Stoodt and Burns, 1978).

The following is an example of an exercise from Grellet's book *Developing Reading Skills* (1981):

> *Specific aim:* To train the students to use the text on the back of a book, the preface and the table of contents to get an idea of what the book is about.
>
> *Skills involved:* Reference skills.
>
> *Why?* It is often important to be able to get a quick idea of what a book is about (e.g. when buying a book or choosing one in the library). Besides, glancing through the book, the text on the back cover, in the preface and in the table of contents gives the best idea of what is to be found in it.
>
> (Grellet, 1981)

Many American books aimed at teachers give detailed information on the skills to be attained by each grade level, and these same skills, they suggest, are achieved by using the structural guiders. It must be pointed out here that many American schools teach the use of structural guiders as specific sub-skills: there is a proliferation of books in the States, including both textbooks for students and texts for teachers, which aim to help develop these sub-skills.

All the work quoted so far suggests that structural guiders are of a great importance. Let us look more closely now at the importance of each individual guider. I give below the results of my research into the structural guiders provided in children's information books.

The book cover

The importance of the book cover for a survey has long been recognised by the supporters of SQ3R (Robinson, 1962; Walker, 1974; Orlando, 1979). The front of the book should have a well chosen title and the layout and illustrations should suggest to the reader what the book might be about.

In a well designed book the writing on the back cover should tell the reader the gist of the book. It might give the chapter headings and it might also tell the reader a little about the author. The cover blurb is a form of advance organiser, telling the reader what the book is going to be about. Publishers should be more keen to provide this useful feature rather than using the back of the book as an advertisement for other books: only 38% of all the books surveyed had relevant information on the reverse. All the same, it does seem that the covers of recently published books are offering more helpful advice to young readers.

Index

Indexes are recognised as an important tool by all teachers, librarians and researchers alike. They give the reader a means by which to locate and extract specific information.

One would have thought that indexes would be a standard feature of children's informative texts, but this is not so: only 58% of the books in my survey had one. Even those books I analysed that did have indexes, often had ones which lacked the detail and the arrangement which pupils need to help them find the relevant sections. Indexes varied in their layout, and no advice was given to readers on how to use the index of each particular book. For example, the use of bold print varies in different indexes, but it is not always obvious what the bold text indicates.

Guidance on how indexes are to be used could well be a beneficial feature in some books. But children also need to be taught index skills. They need to know, for instance, that an index is arranged alphabetically, that each entry can refer to more than one page, that entries consist of key words, and that entries can be cross-referenced.

Educationalists often forget that indexes are difficult to use, and that they as adults have been continually improving their skill in the use of indexes. Children have to realise for example that the absence of a topic from an index is no guarantee of its exclusion from the text.

Although just over half of the books in my survey had an index, having an index was not a good guide to the usefulness of the book. I found that some indexes were very unhelpful. Many of them include entries for passing references to words. I have found that indexes like this, in fact, often do more harm than good because children make the enormous effort of finding the entry and then they cannot do anything constructive with the information that they are given.

Looking up words in an index is laborious and it is postulated that fewer references for a particular word might help young readers. Certainly, references to mere mentions of words, should not be included. I also found some indexes where the words were not in correct alphabetical order.

Introduction/preface/foreword

Children need introductions because they help them to assess what the book is about and to plan to read appropriately. In this study it was found that less than half the books had introductions (43%) and, of those that did have introductions, very few were written for the intended audience (children). In most cases the introductions were quite clearly written for an adult or the teacher.

Introductions have been found to be useful tools for readers for as James McCallister (1964) states,

> the introductory statements that are found frequently at the begin-
> nings of selections are valuable in giving the reader a mental set, that
> aids greater interpretation. Such statements usually give the purpose
> of the author; they may give a preview of the contents of the
> selection, and they may indicate its plan of organisation. They prepare
> the reader by indicating what he may expect to find in the selection as
> he reads. By using introductory statements as guides to reading, the
> reader comprehends better the intention and exact meaning that the
> author means to convey.
> (McCallister, 1964)

What is important about a good introduction is that it alerts the reader to what to expect. An 'advance organiser' is a more sophisticated form of introduction. I shall now explain what an advance organiser is and how they work, as I think that one at the beginning of a non-narrative book would greatly help young readers.

Advance organisers

An advance organiser is intended to help readers to associate new learning with prior knowledge. It is a piece of text introducing the main body of written material. It tells readers what they will be reading, why, and what they will know at the end of the read. Ausubel (1968) says

> The principal function of the organizer is to bridge the gap between
> what the learner already knows and what he needs to know before
> he can successfully learn the task in hand.
> (Ausubel, 1968)

An advance organiser might even suggest to the reader what reading approach to take. In the words of Tonjes (1986): 'the purpose of an advance organiser is to provide a scaffolding or framework prior to reading'. Advance organisers have been found to be very effective. Rothkopt (1965, 1982) and Ausubel (1968, 1978) have both found that these pre-reading strategies enhance comprehension. It is interesting that advance organisers use the reader's prior knowledge and try to bring it to mind before the reading activity commences. As Ausubel says, advance organisers draw upon and mobilise the relevant anchoring concepts which are already established in the learner's cognitive structure. The advance organisers make these active and ongoing which makes the new material more familiar and potentially more meaningful.

It will be remembered that only 43% of the books surveyed had an introduction. None of the introductions that were found had the features of an advance organiser. Yet it seems that the features of an advance organiser would be a great help to young readers. If books did have these features, teachers could also help the children to identify which parts of the book to read. The advance organisers would also show them how to make best use of the book.

Rowntree (1988) has pointed out that for open learning purposes a book must have a list of aims and objectives and a flow chart showing how the ideas in the various chapters connect with each other. He also suggests that a list of new concepts to be introduced is included, together with clear statements as to the relevance of what is being presented. Clearly he is suggesting features of advance organisers. If editors insisted on a really well-planned advance organiser it might not be quite so important for the main body of text to be so well set out.

To summarise, an introduction should explain what the book is about, the main features to look out for, how the book is organised and how the book might be used. This feature should be included in most informative books for children since in my view it would probably help immature readers as much as it does more experienced readers.

Table of contents

Contents pages in informative books have a different function from those in narrative books. In a novel, the contents page is designed not to tell the reader too much about the story, but just enough to whet the appetite. In a non-narrative book, the contents should give as much information as possible. I think this difference between the uses should be made clear to children. I have found very few children who recognise the differences on their own.

Most study skill manuals mention the importance of looking at a table of contents to obtain the gist of a book. An efficient reader turns to the table of contents to see what the author proposes to talk about and in what order. Brunner and Campbell (1976) suggest that a contents page tells you where a trip begins and their advice to their readership (secondary pupils) is

> Think of it as a map of the book . . . Without a table of contents the reader has very little idea of what topics the author is likely to cover.
> (Brunner and Campbell, 1976)

The percentage of books in my survey containing a table of contents was 61%. This is low, considering that this is such an important guider. In my view, children need contents pages that are uncluttered. Some tables of contents are so poorly laid out that they are very crowded and it is difficult to distinguish important information from detail.

Often the language is difficult, specialist or detailed, making the contents page difficult to use. It would be beneficial to young readers if the layout and wording of the table of contents were to gain more attention from editors than it does at present.

Headings

A number of study skills manuals expand upon the importance of looking at the headings as a good initial strategy. Headings alert the reader to what is to come. Some research, including that of Foster and Coles (1977) and Crouse and Idstein (1972) suggests that typographical cues for highlighting can help readers find and remember information. The work of Jenkins and Bailey (1964) suggests, however, that too much highlighting can be detrimental. Dooling and Lachman (1971) found that the presence of a thematic title, or a title that told the readers what the text was going to be about, increased recall by 18% compared with a text that had no useful heading. The research of Anderson, Spiro and Anderson (1978), Bransford and Johnson (1972), Dansereau, Brooks, Spurlin and Holley (1979), Charrow (1988) and Schallert and Kleinman (1979) all suggests that headings and titles can be very helpful to the reader. I found from my research that as many as 29% of the books had no headings or bold print yet these should be the clues which help the reader to search for information.

Interestingly, 39 books had headings even though they had no contents page, so these would be more helpful than those with neither. Even more surprising is the fact that 17 books had a contents page but had no headings or bold print!

Headings should be closely related to the text beneath them. If the main heading is, for example, *deep water*, the text beneath it should not concern canals, which are shallow waterways. All sub-headings should also relate to deep water and not, for example, water sports or fish. Editors should ensure that the main heading on a page does not mislead as to the contents of that page. If the main heading on a double page spread is *Pollution*, the whole spread should relate to pollution: there should not be sub-headings, and sub-section of text, dealing with unconnected issues.

Another finding was that some books probably had too many headings.

Some had headings every twenty-five words. In these books the readability level was very low (see pages 79–85), but books of this nature give the reader very little to engage with. In light of this work and other research on headings it is clear that this aspect of children's books needs more thought. Expository texts would probably be easier to read if the text were broken up into reasonably small units so that readers could select what they wanted to read. How small the unit of text should ideally be is a question requiring further research.

Just how useful headings can be to young readers will be seen in Chapter 8. They can learn how to reject text by designing their own headings but, more importantly, they can learn to use the headings as an active question (see page 141).

Illustrations

The importance of illustrations is widely acknowledged in work on learning to read. For instance, Smith (1972), McKenzie and Warlow (1977), Harris and Sipay (1975), and Holdaway (1979) all mention the help that illustrations give to readers trying to understand narrative texts. However, there are not so many references to the importance of illustrations in expository texts. But if they are important in the early stages of narrative reading, they must surely be important in early information books because the reader can then predict what the text might be about. Newton (1983) in a small study on primary children's science texts found that the presence of illustrations can substantially improve children's ability to comprehend these texts. However, Harris and Sipay (1975) pointed out how difficult the use of illustrations can be. He suggests that young readers are not used to lifting their eyes and then re-finding their place in the text, so they find the integration of text and illustrations difficult. He believes that the competent reader can cope with illustrations and text alongside each other but beginner readers need help.

The reading of graphic, tabular and diagrammatic materials has been found to be a particularly difficult task. I have often found that children love to look at the illustrations in books but they need to be taught how to learn from them, especially from diagrams and charts.

Another factor which is often overlooked is that many children's informative books have photographs while most narrative texts have drawings. This is an example of the differences between the two types of books which are obvious to adults but need to be made explicit to young children.

References to illustrations

As many as 35% of the books that I analysed had illustrations with no captions to go with them. Usually in these cases the illustrations were just sketches drawn on the page, slightly obscured by text set on top of them. The aim of these drawings is probably to make the page look less daunting.

Ross (1982) gives some useful guidelines for selecting texts with helpful illustrations. He suggests that the captions must help the reader's understanding and that they should also draw attention to the illustrations and particular features of interest. The illustrations should be clear and should convey accurate information which complements the text, and they should be positioned in such a way that they draw the reader into the text.

By watching children closely I have found that they sometimes do not understand the function of a caption. Sometimes the captions are so badly sited on the page that children read on from the main body of text straight into the caption, without realising that they have done so.

A surprising feature that I have found in some children's books is the inclusion of references to the illustrations within the main body of writing, rather than the inclusion of captions. I think this approach, the use of implicit references to illustrations, makes special demands on the reader. It is discussed in more detail on pages 73–4.

Bibliography

A surprisingly low percentage of books had a bibliography (only 26% of all the books in the survey), but I believe that bibliographies should become a standard feature of children's books. From my experience in the classroom I have found that children like to know which other books to refer to and they find it exciting dealing with two texts that refer to each other.

The value of bibliographies is not so widely acknowledged as that of the other structural guiders, yet a bibliography does teach the young reader the important idea that authors glean their knowledge and information from other sources. It also gives children who wish to pursue or extend a particular area of knowledge some possible resources to turn to.

Glossary

A glossary is a list of specialist terms with accompanying definitions. Brunner and Campbell (1976) describe a glossary as 'a short dictionary usually found at the end of a text'. It can also be described as a dictionary of 'Stopper words'. It should have in it those specialist words which would otherwise hinder the reader because of their unfamiliarity. Many reading manuals and methodology books are recommending that teachers explain the stopper words before asking the children to read the main text.

The percentage of books in my survey that had a glossary was again very low: only 24%. The problem with many of the glossaries that I looked at was that they did not actually help the reader to understand the word in question, because the definitions used specialist, technical vocabulary with which children could not be expected to be familiar.

Williams (1983), in his work in adult texts, drew conclusions similar to my own. He claimed that authors used far too many abstract words and did not explain them fully. It is my view that a book should have a glossary if it is on any subject whose vocabulary might be new to young children. There should also be a standard place for a glossary, be it the back or the front. It should be well signposted and the entries should not be explained using other terms that may also be new to the reader. A glossary requires great thought and care from the author. It must help the reader who has little prior knowledge of the subject.

Summaries/reviews

Not one of the books in my survey contained a summary. Summaries can be in an abstract or abridged form, and can be either at the end of the book or at the end of each chapter. In recent study texts it has been common practice to include reviews at regular intervals throughout the text. This is especially true in American books.

Banton and Smith (1974) have reviewed the research on the effects of the presence or absence of a summary. They found that summaries were useful to serious readers: many methodology books tell their readers to look for summaries or reviews, so that they can consolidate what they have read.

It must not be forgotten that effective readers often read the summary of a text before they read the main body of information. This helps them to set their mind on what the author thinks is important. Indeed, it might be sufficient for the reader just to read the summary and ignore the rest of the work. It is postulated, as a result of my research, that children who may not naturally use such strategies should be introduced to them: they should be taught how to use summaries as part of their reading training.

Teachers may know the usefulness of summaries but they cannot teach children how to use them as an advance organiser or *aide memoire* if they do not appear in the books to which the children have access. Children's books without summaries are failing to give children a good model of expository texts. One of the important objectives of including summaries in young children's books should be to show them that explanations or descriptions can be truncated, and superfluous material cut out, without loss of meaning. In other words, summaries provide working examples for young children of one form of notemaking. This idea will be further developed in Chapter 8.

Figure 3.1 shows a chart summarising my findings from this part of the analysis.

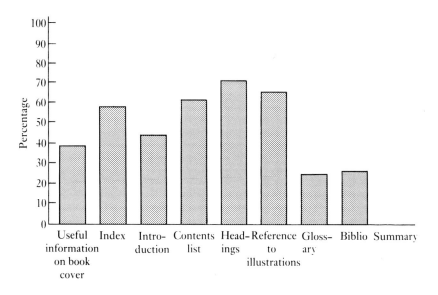

Fig. 3.1 Graph showing the percentage of books surveyed that contained each type of structural guider

ORGANISATION

The First National Curriculum Council Report, commonly known as the Cox Report (1989) stated that children learn how information is logically organised by using information books. I have found that many children's information books are not so well organised as the committee suggested, and that some fail to be logical. Many seem to be hurriedly assembled with little attention paid to the layout or the organisation. Many of the books would be greatly improved if they had a clearer structure.

Research suggests that better organised texts are better remembered (Goetz and Armbruster, 1980; Meyer, 1977, 1984; Meyer, Brandt and Bluth, 1980; Shimmerlik and Nolan, 1976).

Reigeluth and Stein (1983) found that information must be put into manageable logical chunks, and the transition links between the chunks must be made clear. In other words the connections between the various parts of a text must be revealed.

Most research on organisation of informational books has been carried out on books for older students rather than young pupils, but McLaughlin (1966) found that badly designed texts affected poorly motivated students more than they affected keener ones. By the same token I would like to argue that weak organisation may well affect young pupils more than it does older students. More adept readers may know how to deal with poor organisation but young readers are still learning how information books are structured. Again it seems that children's books fail to provide a good model.

Organisation of content

All too often the books I surveyed had confused organisation. For example editors frequently fail to ensure that chapters follows a logical progression. A sequence might go from issues concerning all fish to those concerning individual types of fish, back to fish in general, through to where fish live, and back to individual types of fish. Such a sequence would not teach children anything about the logical presentation of information.

Page layout

Many of the books studied also have confusing page layouts. Many children (and indeed adults) would find it difficult to know where to start reading on a particular page. Sometimes there are numerous little boxes on the page. Sometimes the captions are positioned so that readers read from the main text into the captions.

Designers should ensure that page layouts give guidance on which section should be read first. No prior knowledge of the subjects should be assumed and the page should not be cluttered with distracting boxes or lists. It should be clear which captions relate to which illustrations and captions should not be too long, they should be limited to conveying one idea.

Bold lettering

In many children's books there are words set in bold type apparently for little purpose. If words are set in bold lettering, there should be some logic behind the choice of words so emphasised. Words set in bold should be fully explained.

Prior knowledge

In Chapter 1, prior knowledge was shown to be of great importance to the reader. The extent of prior knowledge assumed in some of the texts I surveyed was surprising.

Take the example of a book on castles: the text should fully explain all specialist vocabulary, it should not assume prior knowledge of the sequence of historical events, or of the development of building technology or of geography. The author should not use familiar words in unfamiliar contexts. The author should also not assume that children will be able to determine the connections between related pieces of text, between illustrations and between text and illustration. Unfortunately, books violating all these prohibitions on the assumption of prior knowledge do still get published.

Concept overload

Reading is the interaction between reader and text and one of the major hurdles of this interaction is that of conceptual difficulty. Texts can be understood at different levels but it can be seen from studies into the importance of prior knowledge that the more one knows about a topic before reading a text, the more likely it is that one will be able to learn from it. A point made by Anderson, Mason and Shirley (1984) is that often the problem is in the concepts involved rather than the text itself. They say:

> Probably most third grade students (eight year olds) could get the gist of a story about a girl and her puppy even if it were dressed up in fancy language whereas no amount of simplification of [the language of] an economics treatise would permit third graders to grasp the concept of multiplier effect.
> (Anderson, Mason and Shirley, 1984)

Pearson, Hansen and Gordon (1979) found that matched second graders who knew a lot about spiders comprehended much more in a text on spiders than a group who knew nothing about spiders. Very often the choice of topic for young children's books has not been wisely made. Authors have often chosen subjects that are just too demanding for young children and that cannot be simplified in a way that will make any sense. *A Wrigley Book About Time* is a good example of difficult concepts being explained in simple language. Time is a very difficult concept and, although the book really does use simple vocabulary, children will only understand it with adult help.

A sample from the text is:

> Being late means you haven't been exact with your timing; being late means you took too long, were too slow in arriving.
> (Wrigley, 1976)

There is also a pun on the word "time" on the last page 'Think some more about time . . . It's time you did!'. These two uses of the word will be lost on many young children.

A spin-off from the simplification of the language is that many books give children so many facts in such few words that they experience a concept overload. There are no redundant words, which makes for very difficult reading and learning. Readers need to be given space and time to think about the new concepts they have met. They must be told of the concepts and knowledge in many different ways so that there is repetition of the notions. This rarely happens and publishers need to become much more sensitive to the problems created by concept overload.

As Davison (1986) so rightly sums up:

> In general the complexity of the ideas being conveyed is what directs the choice of language. Changing the external features of complexity . . . that is sentence length and word difficulty . . . will not necessarily simplify the ideas expressed.
> (Davison, 1986)

Anderson, Armbruster and Kantor (1980) in a comprehensive piece of work suggest that, when texts are written with short sentences the meaning link goes, and hence the reader has the additional problem of inference to cope with. The authors stress that the condensing of ideas, which is often found in books lacking connectives and those texts written to readability formulae, actually means that the text has an increase in the density of the concepts (see Chapters 4 and 5).

Economy

Many of the books surveyed looked as if they had been produced to a tight budget or schedule. Publishers should be prepared to invest more resources in children's information books. Editors should spend more time thinking about the structure of the books they are editing.

Multicultural aspects

It is interesting to note that a number of publishers have tried to exploit the present demand for multicultural books. Many of the newer books which give information about the jobs people do include people who are not white and have non-English names. The problems with these books are that they display some of most extreme features of books that have a mixed reading function. They neither tell a story nor give information in a straightforward manner. Mixed function books are dealt with in more detail on pages 109 and 123.

Capitals

Some writers are confused as to whether to use capitals or not. Some books have proper nouns with no capitals and only use capitals at the start of sentences. In other books the text might have the names of the creatures or plants uncapitalised, while the same names do have capitals in the captions. Editors should be at pains to be consistent in their use of capitals.

Length

During my survey I also looked at the number of words each book had. I came to the conclusion that there is no typical length for a children's information book. The range is vast, from books with 31 words to those with 180,000 words.

It will be seen later that the length of a book tends to increase according to readability formulae (see Chapter 4). Looking at the books individually there are inconsistencies but basically the length of books tends to increase as their readability increases or they become harder. This is logical enough.

In my survey I found that there was a high percentage of very short books. About 45% of the books had fewer than 5,000 words. Yet there were some books with as many as 100,000 words: it is interesting to wonder why librarians and publishers think that such young children should be able to cope with these much longer books.

SUMMARY: STRUCTURE AND ORGANISATION OF CHILDREN'S INFORMATION BOOKS

I argued in Chapter 1 that the structure of information books should be different from that of narrative text. I have also suggested that reading for informative purposes is harder and more demanding than reading narrative text. Children need a great deal of help to enable them to extract information and to learn from texts. My research on information books suggests that children are not being given a useful model on which to learn the strategies of effective and efficient reading. I would now like to divert my reader's attention to the demands of the National Curriculum for I do not think the authors of the English Curriculum realise just how difficult their demands are going to be for teachers and their children. However I would like to make it quite clear here that I do approve of the stress laid on informative reading and I do think the demands will improve the quality of children's learning. But the books must be improved if the children are really going to reap the benefits!

THE NATIONAL CURRICULUM FOR ENGLISH

The National Curriculum demands in relation to informative reading are as follows.

At *Level 1* the children will be 'able to talk in simple terms about the content of information books.'

At *Level 2* the children will be 'able to read a range of material with some independence, fluency, accuracy and understanding.'

At *Level 3* the children will be 'able to devise a clear set of questions that will enable them to select and use appropriate information sources and reference books.'

At *Level 4* the children will be 'able to use simple informational retrieval strategies when pursuing a line of enquiry.'

At *Level 5* the children will be 'able to select reference books and other informational devices e.g. chapter headings, sub-headings etc.'

One of the other demands of the National Curriculum is in the Programmes of Study for Key Stage 1:

> pupils should refer to information books . . . as a matter of course.
> Pupils should be encouraged to formulate first the questions they

> need to answer by using such sources, so that they use them effectively and do not simply copy verbatim.

I will explain further in Chapter 8 what the major difficulties of notemaking are, but at this juncture it is worth summarising just what the National Curriculum demands are. The above extract suggests that children must be able to read books with an 'open learning' approach. They will be expected to work either in groups or as individuals to think up some appropriate questions and then to extract the necessary information from the books. It also suggests that to find the answers to their questions, they will have to be able to use the structural guiders in the books.

The Programmes of Study for Key Stage 2 make this demand more clearly. At Level 4, pupils:

> should be shown how to read different kinds of materials in different ways e.g. search reading to locate a particular fact . . . and how to use list of contents and indexes . . .

At Level 5, the Programmes of Study suggest that pupils should be shown:

> how to make use of organisational devices e.g. chapter headings and sub-headings.

It will be remembered that only 71% of the books in this study had chapter headings, and only 61% of the selected books had contents pages while 58% had indexes. In these circumstances it is clear that teachers are going to have difficulties in teaching children to use such features.

I would also like to suggest that the Level 5 demand is easier than the one at Level 4. From my experience young children find headings and references to illustrations relatively easy to use, while contents lists and indexes require a different type of skill and their use is probably more demanding.

It is clear that most books do not have sufficient structural guiders to make them useful to children, nor do they have organisers of sufficient quality.

A further requirement of the National Curriculum is that children should learn that information is 'logically organised in books' (DES, 1989: 16.25). As has been shown in this chapter, this is not always the case. It is to be hoped that these National Curriculum demands ensure that the quality of children's information books will now improve.

4 Readability

There are many aspects of a text which make it either easy or difficult to read. All of these should be taken into account when assessing its readability. It is important to realise that evaluating the readability of a book essentially means matching the text to the reader. Many formulae have been devised to try to predict objectively how difficult a particular text might be, but we shall find from the following discussion that there are many aspects of texts which are not covered by readability formulae.

In the early days of work on readability it was thought that one might be able to find a perfect formula which would match, for instance, a seven year old with the right text. It is now recognised that reading and readability formulae involve far more complex issues than this. Nevertheless, various ways of trying to match text with reader are worthy of discussion.

METHODS USED IN THE MEASUREMENT OF READABILITY

Readability can be measured by subjective and objective methods. One subjective method is a system whereby teachers or librarians (or both) assess the difficulty of texts based on their experience and on what they think a particular group of children might be able to read. One example of an objective method is a readability formula. A formula uses some sort of word and sentence count to try to match an assumed audience (e.g. 8 year-olds) with a particular text.

A number of readability formulae have been developed, but they all differ slightly in their intentions. Some are better suited to secondary pupils and some to juniors or even infants. Some formulae require mathematical calculations while others use tables or charts. It is important to note that no actual participation by readers is required for readability formulae. This saves the evaluator's time and helps with the problem of access to children, but this strength is also the weakness of readability formulae, for they cannot take into account the interactions between reader and text.

There are a number of problems with readability formulae, the main one being that there are several factors that they cannot measure. These are presented overleaf.

What are the known factors that affect readability?

The factors that affect readability can be put into three categories: first, the production aspects of the book; second, the linguistics of the text, and third, the psychology of the reader. The factors in this third category are very difficult to assess. For instance, the motivation of the reader cannot be assessed by formulae: they do not take into account whether the text is intrinsically useful or interesting to individuals. Yet this is an important factor, since readers can sometimes cope with a text much harder than they could normally read, simply because they really want to read the text. Harrison (1980) calls this the 'Pterodactyl Phenomenon'. Formulae do not take into account the background knowledge and vocabulary that the reader brings to the text either. This is especially important in relation to informative texts.

A further point made by Perera (1979) is that some types of text, such as poetry books, are supported by teacher explanation. Children do not get this sort of help on information texts.

As already mentioned, nearly all readability formulae judge difficulty of texts by word and sentence length. This can be one of their shortcomings, because short words and short sentences do not necessarily make for simpler reading. Harrison's (1980) simple sentence emphasises this point: 'If he is as I am, I am to be as he is.'. This sentence would gain a very low readability score if assessed using a formulae, but it is almost impossible to understand. Thus readability formulae cannot judge whether a text is sensible or easy to understand. Long sentences in themselves do not automatically mean a high readability. Indeed, it is important to remember that short sentences do not necessarily help when explanations are required. Nelson (1978) found that explanations of complex concepts often needed longer sentences in order to preserve important meaning relations.

Perera makes clear in her work that there are frequent instances of pupils understanding all the constituent sentences of a passage and yet not understanding the relationship between them. The children are not understanding the point that is being made. (Further examples of this are included in Chapter 8.) These aspects of a text cannot be put into a formula. The fact that children can read a text out loud, as mentioned previously, does not mean they can understand it.

Certain writers and publishers have taken the findings of research on readability to mean that using short sentences and short common words will make a text suitable for a certain age group. Writing according to readability formulae became widespread in the 1970s and it is still valued by a large number of publishers despite contrary evidence.

For instance, some studies have shown that readability is not necessarily improved by simplified editions. These, as will be seen in the next chapter, are certainly no easier to extract information from (Charrow and Charrow, 1979; Chall, 1958; Klare, 1976; Anderson and Davison, 1986). Often simplified editions leave out connectives. These omissions have created an area of disagreement amongst educationalists as to whether connectives are helpful or difficult for young readers. It seems from recent research (Davison, 1986) that simplified editions are less coherent, especially in the area of between-sentence connectives. Readers do not understand a text so well when it contains sequences of short, implicitly connected sentences. Perera (1981) claimed that it is possible for young readers to understand individual sentences perfectly and yet fail to grasp the meaning of a whole discourse. She believes that this may be because they do not recognise the connections between the sentences. As was seen in Chapter 1, there are fewer cohesive ties in non-fictional texts, which again makes them more difficult to understand, and the fact that readability formulae do not count or analyse connectives means that this aspect of non-fictional texts totally eludes them.

It seems from Sutton's (1981) work that children are perceptive to what makes a text difficult. He carried out an interesting experiment where the children were asked to rewrite a text that they found difficult. Their rewrite was easier for fellow pupils to follow than the adults attempt at rewriting.

Readability formulae therefore have great problems, but in the words of the expert, Klare, they:

> are merely good indices of difficulty. Consequently, altering word or sentence length themselves, can provide no assurance of improving readability. How to achieve more readable writing is another and much more complex endeavour.
> (Klare, 1975–5)

It must be reiterated here that reading is now understood to be an interaction process between the characteristics of the texts and the reader. Readability research must take this into account.

READABILITY: MY FINDINGS

The Fry graph (figure 4.1) overleaf has been recognised as a valid and reliable means of assessing readability, and is frequently used for the age group to which my study applied. It is actually effective across the entire school age range (5–16 years) and it is also easy to use.

Use of the Fry graph involves calculating the number of sentences per hundred words and the number of syllables per hundred words in a given text. The results are then plotted on a graph which yields an approximate US grade level. To calculate an approximate reading age in years, one adds five to the result. This technique was used in my research. I looked at three hundred books and analysed their readability according to this graph.
The following findings were made.

1   The readability of the children's information books in the study was high according to the measures used. The mean readability level across all of the books in the sample was 11.37 years according to the Fry readability graph. This seems very high, considering that the books collected were for children aged 7–11: the average readability of the books was higher than the top age group found in the junior school. This suggests that most of the books placed in school libraries for project work are too hard for their readers. The findings support those that were made by Lunzer and Gardner (1979), but their research

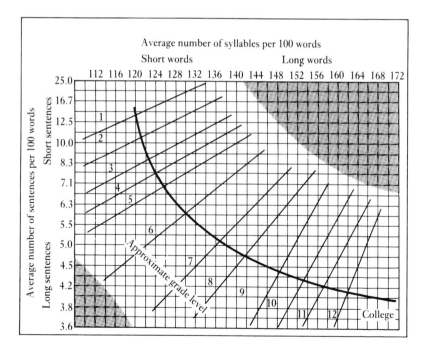

Fig. 4.1   Fry readability graph

looked at books for secondary rather than primary children. The findings also support the subjective feelings of many primary teachers.

2   Looking at the figures in a different manner, it can be seen that only a third of the books fell within the 7–11 range according to the readability graph. The other books were either in the very simple range, or were too hard. The graph in figure 4.2 below, shows this.

   The graph shows that most of the books in the study were suitable for children in the 10–12 year age group. Yet these are books designed for and used by 7–11 year-olds.

3   The research also suggests that books designed for 7–11 year-olds might have a range of readabilities from the Fry 5 year-old to the Fry 18 year-old. Children might therefore pick up, in the course of their project work, a book which according to readability formulae is suitable for a reception class. On the other hand they might just as easily pick up a book that is suitable for an educated adult. A typical project pack of

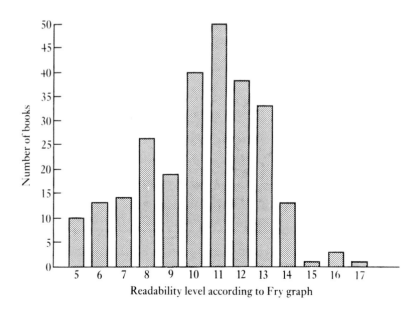

Fig. 4.2   Graph showing the number of books at each readability level

books from this study would have this sort of diversity of readability. The difference in the readability of a book assessed at the 5 year-old level and one assessed at the 18 year-old level is vast: it must be very perplexing for these young readers.

4   It was found that some topics had higher mean readability levels than others, the difference being as much as 2.5 years. For instance the books on Romans were found to be harder than those on animals.

5   The books published more recently tended to have a lower readability level. The range of the readabilities for these books is therefore becoming less wide.

6   Generally speaking, most of the books that had no structural guiders had a lower readability level. Those books which had introductions, chapter headings, references to illustrations or bibliographies, were more likely to have a much higher readability score.

7   When I analysed the dates of publication of the books, I discovered a trend towards publishing shorter books.

8   As will be seen in Chapter 5, a large number of the books were written to readability guidelines which probably made them no easier to read, and in many cases made them harder.

Conclusions

I have suggested that readability formulae do have failings and that they are particularly weak when used on informational texts because they cannot take into account the prior knowledge factor, that is the level of prior knowledge that each pupil brings to the text. It also seemed that a large number of the texts in the study were written to readability guidelines which probably made them no easier to read.

I do not think that the readability results reported here should be taken too seriously, for two reasons.

1   Readability formulae are clearly not so good for informative texts because the prior knowledge factor is not taken into account – see Activity 3 on p. 29. I believe that many children can read these books aloud or appear to understand them when in fact they do not.

2   I have found that as long as a piece of text is well written and the aim is to impart knowledge, its readability level as evaluated by formula has little relevance. What matters is the ability of the author to select and place words so that the reader can learn. These further language issues will be discussed in Chapters 5 and 6. It will be seen in Chapter 8 that many of the activities work better with texts that have a real message for the reader, even though they may have a higher readability score than those texts that try to simplify.

5 Register

The last two chapters showed the books in the study to be diverse in terms of their degree of structure and organisation and their readability. This is no less true in the case of register. However, it is important to probe further into these books by looking more closely at their language.

As discussed in Chapter 1, studies on reading suggest that most primary children learn to read on narrative registers. Their first experience of informational registers is when they read as part of their project work. In my study I considered whether the clash of registers mentioned by both Lunzer and Gardner (1979) and Chapman and Louw (1986) may start not when children transfer from primary to secondary school, but in the primary school itself. Primary children are not only exposed to the registers of specialist subjects, but they are also faced with an array of registers. Some of these registers are intended to help the reader, but it is possible that they actually hinder the reader.

THE DIVERSITY OF TEXTS

The work of Halliday and Hasan (1976, 1978, 1980) suggests that there are three features of any context that shape the nature of the language in a text. They are termed *field*, *tenor* and *mode*. These three together make up the *register* of the text. The register of a text will depend on its purpose and content just as our spoken language depends upon the situation in which we are using it.

REGISTER RECOGNITION

It has already been mentioned that adults must have a bank of registers to enable them to operate as communicators. Adults need only three or four phrases to be able to identify a register. Hasan (1980) gives as examples of opening text, phrases such as 'Once upon a time', 'In the beginning' and 'Dear sir': once read, these phrases alert the reader to a certain register.

To illustrate this even more clearly, Raleigh (1981) gives short, easily identifiable examples of various kinds of writing.

John was not the only boy involved but it seems to me that since his was the leading role in this unfortunate incident I must . . .

It came slowly towards the crowd, its eyes glaring, its teeth bared. The people in the crowd stood stock-still, frozen with fear while . . .

And so it came to pass that on the fourth day men, women and children came out of the city into the valley below and . . .

I am 16 years of age and just about to leave school after taking CSE examinations. I am interested . . .

To release the cylinder block, first slacken off the camshaft chain tensioner. Then unscrew and remove the single bolt at the rear . . .

Now when the little dwarf heard that he was to dance a second time before the queen he was so proud that . . .

With their album already flying high, the band are planning a number of gigs . . .
(Raleigh, 1981)

From these short written extracts one can draw conclusions about the context from which they came. Spoken language also has a range of registers. It is important to realise that all written or spoken language has a register, whether the text is long or short, basic or literary, factual or fictional. All language fits into one register or a combination of registers.

There are some easily recognisable registers such as that of the conversation between a mother and child on topics like getting ready for bed, playing on the swings and brushing one's teeth. There is also the fairy story register. Out and about there is the register of the market stall, which will vary slightly from that of the conversation at the smarter greengrocer down the road. There is even a children's party register where there are certain norms: the children will be very likely to say 'thank you for having me'. Meeting the doctor is another example. We have all experienced this, so we can all imagine what the doctor might say. It must be stressed that it is our knowledge of the situation that helps us to understand what is going on. In oral language we do not have to state the context because the clues are all around us. In written texts the context has to be made explicit, for we have to imagine the situation if it is not obvious from clues given to us by the author. It is thought that children have difficulty with the written word because they require these additional situational clues. They cannot understand a text unless they know something about the context in which it occurs.

Texts vary in their purposes and meanings and according to whether they are informative or not. For instance, the narrative text of fairy stories has its own structure and organisation which is very different from that of newspaper reports or car repair manuals. Young children are used to books having a story grammar. Expository texts do not have this (see Chapter 2). The culture of the situation is also important, because (for example) going to the dentist would not necessarily be the same in all cultures.

Each register uses different words and language structures and it is these two features that enable the reader to readily assess the situation of the text. In the terminology of systemic linguistics registers create and use field, mode and tenor. In this study the first 500 words of each book were used to analyse its registers. From this limited number of words one cannot get a full picture of all the registers used throughout each book but, as Hasan suggests, one can get a good clue as to the type of language used in the rest of the book.

REGISTER CHANGE

It is important to point out that texts do not fit neatly into distinct packages according to their register. Hasan says:

> Registers do not begin and end suddenly. There is no such thing as one clearly defined register which is different from all others.
> (Hasan, 1980)

She continues:

> I reject the assumption that it is possible for us to seal off the boundaries of one register totally from any other.
> (Hasan, 1980)

The problem relevant to this study is that within a text, registers do change – they are not absolutes. As will be explained later, it was found that children's books probably changed register even more frequently than adult texts.

It is also important to state here that registers within a category or 'group of registers' very often vary. In some instances the variation is slight: often it is only by a matter of degree that two texts differ. This leads me on to the notion of clines.

Clines

A cline was defined by Margaret Berry in 1975 to be 'A scale on which all the points shade into each other'. At one end of the cline the language is quite different from the other but in between there is a continuous spectrum of language. The changes from one end to the other are gradual. The differences between one category and the next cannot necessarily be identified. Clines are continual, to show that language changes from one end to the other, fixed points or groups are identified along the continuum.

The cline is a concept used by systemic linguists. This school of linguistics sees language as having so complex an existence that it will not fall exactly into cut and dried categories. Categories of language can be created but not all examples fit neatly into them: there are always exceptions to whatever categories are defined. Systemic linguists see the edges of a category to be so blurred that one category fades into another.

In this study there are two major groupings of language: the formal and the informal. They occur at opposite ends of the continuum as shown in figure 6.1 on page 95. Within the continuum there are finer divisions, each of which fades into the next. Some types of language can now be identified and put at either end of a continuum, though as has already been pointed out, there are no hard and fast rules.

CHILDREN'S WRITING

Some of the children's texts, identified later, have features in common with children's early writing. It is important to consider whether there is a good reason for this.

There are some basic differences between written and spoken registers (Perera 1984, 1986, 1987). Much research has demonstrated that we actually use language in different ways when we speak and when we write. Sentence structure, for instance, is very different: indeed, we don't use sentences very often in spoken language but we nearly always do in written work.

An important point to make in relation to this study is the fact that, in a spoken situation, it is unnecessary to explain the context. The participants usually know the situation and the language is often vague and not explicit. Children find it difficult to transfer from spoken to written language for, when writing, children have to learn to assume that the reader knows nothing of the context. Children find this process of divorcing themselves from the immediate and putting themselves in the place of the reader very demanding.

Because written and spoken language have basic register differences, Kress (1982) has stated that 'Learning to write has the same features as learning a second language'. In other words there are conventions of written text that have to be learnt. Children have problems with writing different registers, and Kress (1982) identifies some of these. He postulates first that children may have little idea of the mode of written language and second that they may have little idea of the register of expository texts. Children do not appreciate that expository texts do not have beginnings, middles and ends. Children who are learning to write expository texts have to learn to use 'to be' and 'to have' and the general pronoun 'you'. Children's writing, Kress observes, is full of the pronoun 'I' and tends to use the universal present tense, which implies that the actions or events happen at all times and not at particular times. Kress believes there should be more emphasis in schools on understanding the different types of registers, for clearly the various registers make different demands.

The National Curriculum (1990, 1991) demands that more stress be put on learning to write in an appropriate mode for an intended audience. We all have occasion to construct written text for different purposes and audiences, so it makes sense that this skill should be taught. The problem is that in most primary schools the narrative text is still given greater prominence than other texts.

In the early years of education, the teacher often seeks and values written expressions of the child's personal opinion and attitude. Yet as Rothery (1984) has pointed out, such expressions are not a feature of mature writing. In other words, teachers are encouraging the children to obtain a skill which they will have to change in order to become proficient writers.

A study of young children's writing by Rothery (1984) suggests that before children learn to write narratives their work consists of 'recounts'. A recount is a piece of text that retells an event, such as 'we went to the seaside and I fell in the water'. Rothery's work is interesting because many of the texts that have been studied in this survey are more like recounts than narratives. Nothing happens in these texts: there are no complications. Although written for children, these texts provide a poor model for children's writing. Consequently the children, when doing their own writing, know no better than to copy the model provided by the book.

CHILDREN'S READING DIET

As pointed out in Chapter 1, research findings suggest that children are inadequately prepared for the change of reading diet that they experience when they reach secondary school. At this stage there is a register clash that is characterised by a lack of familiarity with written text registers (Lunzer and Gardner, 1979; Merritt, 1978; Chapman and Louw, 1986; Perera, 1984).

The 'register shock' is an idea put forward originally by Lunzer and Gardner (1979). They suggested that the types of texts met in primary and secondary schools are so different that this could be one reason why children of transitional age 'retreat from print'. Littlefair's research (1991) has suggested that children's understanding of register develops slowly. She classified the types of text that 9 year-old and 15 year-old children experience into four groups: literary, expository, reference and procedural.

Spiro and Taylor (1980) claimed in their research that children had great difficulty changing from narrative texts to expository texts, and also found that their work was hampered by the hazy distinction between these two registers. Fry (1985) found that books with 'hazy' registers actually caused confusion in the reader's minds:

> There are times when our need for information is uppermost in our motives as readers. There are times, too, especially in schools, when information books pretend to be stories, and when stories are thought only good for the information they contain. The readers in this study hardly comment at all upon this kind of learning as one of their satisfactions from stories. Not surprisingly for if we look for facts in stories, then we do not read them as fiction.
> (Fry, 1985)

I found a number of hazy registers in the children's information books that I studied, and certainly my work suggests that children find these more difficult than clear cut registers. An information text, in my view, must be written so that the reader can learn.

Perera in 1979 suggested that if children are faced with unfamiliar subject matter, plus technical vocabulary, plus demanding sentence structure, then 'the chances of full comprehension are much reduced'. She stressed that readers will need support in informational reading, because:

> Unaided they will experience frustration and failure, which may lead them to reject academic reading altogether.
> (Perera, 1979)

Donaldson (1988) agrees with Perera and suggests that the degree of impersonality in expository writing is a matter of style, at least to some extent. However she clearly thinks that impersonal language can be overdone:

I reject the exaggeration which holds it improper to say "I" or "in my opinion" when writing on an impersonal theme.
(Donaldson, 1988)

Nevertheless, Donaldson does accept that the impersonal turns of phrase like 'one reason' or 'the cause of this seems to be' can help the writing of expository prose.

REGISTER: MY FINDINGS

The research concentrated on the following issues.

1   How many different registers do primary children experience when reading information books?

2   Are there, at this primary level, different registers in the different topic areas, and are subject areas of registers introduced in primary texts?

3   Within one of the chosen topic areas, what diversity of register is there?

4   Are there texts that abruptly and erratically change register in mid-stream?

5   Can a cline be identified that has informative text at one end and narrative at the other?

6   Can a cline of formality be identified?

7   Are there features of a text that help to classify it into a particular register?

8   Is there an identifiable register used in simplified books?

The Classification of the registers from the selected texts

The first 500 words (approximately) were taken from the beginning of each of the 282 books. It is recognised that, as the sample was taken from the beginning of each book, the text in it may not be a true reflection of the registers of the whole book. However, it is the part of the book that many children will start to read first, even though this is not necessarily a good strategy when tackling information books. So the first few words of a text give the young reader a feeling as to the sort of register that is to follow.

Each sample of 500 words was analysed to see if the text could be put into a register category of some sort. The choice of register category had, to some extent, to be subjective: it was not easy to decide which text fitted into which category, and some of the texts could have fitted into two or more.

As was discussed earlier in this chapter, it is not surprising that some texts are difficult to classify because registers are expected by their very nature to change within a text. In this study, some extracts of text were relatively easy to classify because they belonged to traditional subject areas, for example History. But there were a surprising number that did not fit into either a subject category or the didactic informational category. Some of the texts seemed to alter register so often and so erratically that it was almost impossible to put them into a category.

A separate category was created for these texts, and I called it the Erratic Registers category. Other texts that were difficult to classify were those that had many questions throughout the text, and those that used numerous implicit references to the illustrations. Thus a category was created for both these two groups as well. It must be realised, though, that the categories into which texts were placed are not necessarily fully representative of the 500 words and are even less representative of each whole book.

Synopsis

I found that there are basically two classes of register – the formal and the informal. The formal tended to be more specialist and the informal more non-specialist. The formal texts were all didactic but varied in tenor (the social distance between author and reader). The tenor varied a great deal but even within each category of registers it was possible to identify formal and less formal registers. The registers could be divided into a number of sub-categories starting with the most formal. These were:

1   Subject area registers. The ones recognised in the study were Historical, Geographical, Botanical, Naturalistic (of Natural History) and Scientific.

2   Other registers that are commonly found in adult texts were also found in this study: these were Autobiographical, Guide-book, Identification Key-guide and Biographical.

3 Types of text were also identified, the most common being Descriptive Process (a system of operations, a series of actions, changes); Recipes (a formula for cooking); Instructional Manual (read and do something as a result of the read), and Exercise Books.

4 In addition, registers that are not frequently found in adult texts were identified: these registers seemed peculiar to children's information books. They are as follows:

Erratic: a group of texts that do not seem to have a main register. They change register so frequently and abruptly that they suggest register diversity.

Narrative: three types were recognised: didactic, false and straight narrative. These often changed the function of the text.

Implicit references to the illustrations: those texts that did not have captions but made references to the pictures throughout the main text.

Questioning texts: those that asked numerous questions but often did not give any answers.

6 The variety of registers found in children's information books

By giving the reader many examples of text, this chapter shows the enormous variety that is present in children's information books. The texts have been ordered and put on a cline of formality: at one end of the cline is formal specialist language, and at the other end is informal non-specialist language. The formality of the language, or the social distance between the author and the reader, was the major factor in the positioning of text on the cline.

Figure 6.1 below, shows a model of the cline of formality used in the research. It is a cline of registers found in children's information books. Towards the left are the most formal texts and towards the right are the most informal. The texts to the left of the page are more specialist than the texts to the right. It appears that specialist texts tend to be more formal.

The model shows that the Identification Key Guide registers were found to be the most specialist ones in this study. Texts with these registers were found to use the language of a particular subject area, with specialist conventions. Moving along the continuum, the next registers are the

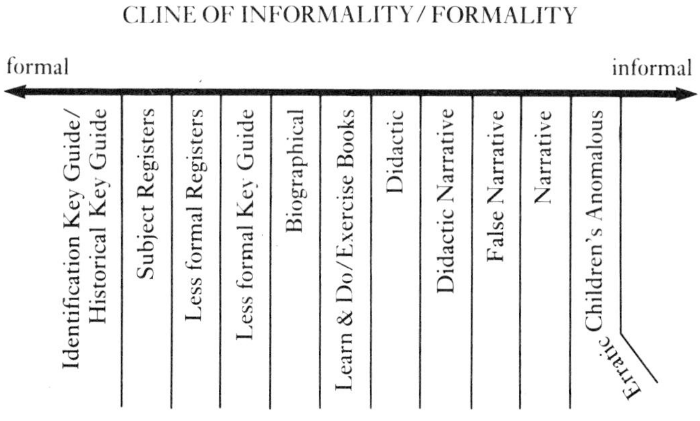

CLINE OF INFORMALITY / FORMALITY

Fig. 6.1   Cline of informality/formality

specific languages of the subject areas identified. Next in the cline are the 'Less Formal Guides'. These are followed by the first of the more familiar registers for primary aged children, the Biographies. Further to the right are the Didactic texts. These are written with the intention of informing, but without using the conventions of a particular subject. The three types of Narrative come next on the cline. They are less formal than the informational texts. Last of all come the three categories of Children's Anomalous Register. These were the least specialist and the least formal.

One example of each of the categories is given below to illustrate the nature of the texts in each category.

IDENTIFICATION KEY GUIDE

There is a very common and clear-cut register associated with books about Nature: it has been called 'Identification Key Guide'. One can find this register in Botany or Zoology texts and it can vary in its formality. The features of these text types are that they have very short sentences and do not use connectives. Neither do they use pronouns, or many function words, but there is frequent use of ellipsis. The texts usually follow a format that is found in academic works. These types of book are often available in schools, and are used especially when children are identifying specimens that they have collected.

> During the summer the fruits are to be found; the capsules, which are not so large as those of other species of this genus, are on setae of about an inch in length and they are four angled.
> (The Observer's Book of Mosses and Liverworts)

The 'Observer's' series of books are common enough in primary schools, although they are not specifically written for children. In this sample there are numerous technical words such as *capsules*, *genus*, and *setae*. Note how this type of text says *about an inch in length*, not *they are one inch long*. The sentence structure is very complicated.

HISTORICAL GUIDE

This register is reminiscent of the language used in guide books.

> The site was well chosen, approachable by land from the south-west

and guarded at that point by two solid bastions beyond the single gate
with its two rectangular guard rooms set back.
(British Castles, Sorrell)

This sample shows the economy of words in such guides. The meaning is
dependent on the internal references made in the text. It is very difficult to
read. Nevertheless children do meet this type of text, usually when books
have been written by experts in a particular field.

SUBJECT REGISTERS

Historical

Texts which have a historical register often use the field words of History
such as the temporal connectives *first*, *later*, *two hundred years ago*, and *in the
beginning*. The frequent mention of dates and the words such as *settlers*,
kings, and *Romans* used to describe groups of people, together with phrases
such as *the area we know now as* give the texts a historical feel.

There are certain words that are found commonly only in historical texts.
All have a particular meaning: *expelling*, *rebelling*, *conquering*, *Fifth Century*,
class of people, *ruled*, *defence*. The reader has to come to grips with all of these
words. It is interesting to see how the National Curriculum for History is
demanding a large historical vocabulary, including for instance *invaders*,
settlers, *civilisation*. The distinctive grammatical features of these registers
are the use of the past tense, and the use of words that describe events that
occurred in the past or to describe structures such as castles. Most of the
texts that have a formal historical register concern themselves with groups
of people rather than individuals.

Assumed prior knowledge seems to be a general feature of historical
texts, yet it should be remembered that many readers may not have been
given any introduction to the subject or any contextual teaching. They
therefore have no previous knowledge of the subject and are coming to the
book cold.

By the beginning of the Fifth Century BC the little villages that had
gradually formed on the Esquiline, Palatine and Quiral had grown and
united into a more compact community enclosed by the defensive
wall attributed to the king.
(Everyday Life in Ancient Rome, Cowell)

This extract is just one long sentence, and the prior knowledge required to
understand its meaning is very great. Children would have to know what

the author means by *Fifth Century* and *BC*, as well as the fact that *Esquiline*, *Palatine* and *Quiral* are hills. The use of the words *gradually formed* is unusual and suggests that they had built themselves. This misleading style is reinforced by the use of *had grown* which again suggests they grew without any human help. The words *compact, community, enclosed, defensive, attributed*, all have specialist meanings that must be understood. Then there is mention of *the king*: which king? Will the reader know?

Geographical

The specialist field word used in geographical texts were those such as *mass, theories, continental drift, earth, crust, ridge, axis, land, landscape* and *mountain*. There does not seem to be any grammatical feature that is particularly characteristic of geographical texts. On the whole it seems to be the field words that make the register identifiable.

> Pompeii was built on a ridge of volcanic rock. The South edge of this ridge drops sharply and made a good defensive position. . . . The Greek were quick to exploit the wealth of the land found around Pompeii. They used the town as a harbour. . . .
> (Pompeii, Andrews)

This extract has a definite geographical approach: many field words are used in this small sample, such as *ridge, volcanic, south, edge* and *harbour*. Much prior knowledge is assumed: I have found that the children do not understand the phrase *the wealth of the land*. Some do not understand the word *harbour* in this context.

Botanical/Natural

Nature is a well established subject in primary schools, and many of the other academic sciences come under this umbrella term. The field words or specialist words of Botany seem to be the names of plants and animals, both in Latin and English, but there is variation in the number and type of other technical words used. Specific descriptions of parts often use technical words such as *buds, stamens, species*, and sometimes even more difficult technical words such as *clusters*. The formality of the language varies according to the purpose of the book: this does not necessarily happen in the other registers.

> The case for state support to conserve wildlife cannot be made entirely on scientific grounds. Legislation to protect our birdlife bylaws, to prohibit the picking of wild flowers and the establishment

of particular areas of country as nature reserves are motivated as much by a desire to preserve an important part of our national heritage as for reasons for research and education.
(Nature Reserves and Wildlife, Duffey)

This text is very difficult to read. The second sentence is 47 words long. There is much to hold in the memory, because all of the second sentence connects back to the first sentence – all of the words are an extension of the words *scientific grounds*. There is much use of specialist terms such as *conserve*, *preserve* and *national heritage*.

Scientific texts

Academic scientific texts have a very specific and formal register, but no examples of it were found in the sample. Some less formal scientific registers were found. Scientific registers were taken in my study to be those which tried to extend children's knowledge, while Didactic registers were those that tried to ensure that readers understood.

Scientific writing has often been analysed because it is quite distinctive and is therefore easier to categorise than other sorts of writing. Davies and Greene (1984) feel that the organisation of scientific texts is of paramount importance, because scientific writers have little choice with the subject matter. There are no opposing views of scientific theories at primary level.

The extracts which have been classified as Scientific are very much 'watered down' compared with academic scientific texts. They do not use the specialised tenor that is widely used in scientific work to distance the writer from the reader, though they do use some scientific field words. Many of the extracts have cause and effect sentences and there are a number of hypothetical phrases beginning with *if* in the texts. These are constructions which are often found in adult scientific registers.

Often the extracts include clear-cut statements. Some of the texts follow an instructional format, while others ask questions and provide the answers.

Have you ever watched a boiling kettle? The bubbling water rattles the lid and sends the steam from the spout. If the kettle is left to boil for a long time the kitchen windows become steamy and the walls wet.
(Rivers, Slack)

This extract gives a question and then proceeds to give an explanation. The *if* makes the register scientific.

> When the very hot vapour rushes out of a kettle spout it mixes with the air in the kitchen and cools into a visible cloud of steam. This is called condensing and it means that the tiny droplets are packed together more and more until they start to join each other. . . .
> Sometimes clouds come down very low or form close to the ground. When this happens it is called mist or fog. As well as invisible gases. . . .
> (Water and Weather, Updegraff)

This is an interesting text: it introduces the word *gases* towards the end, with no previous use of the word. The reader has to be able to infer that the *clouds* and *steam* are the same as vapour which in turn is referred to as an invisible gas. Unless one has the prior knowledge of what a gas is, the inference would be difficult to make.

LESS FORMAL SUBJECT REGISTERS

Less Formal Historical

From many of the texts it seems that writers recognise that a full formal historical text is not always appropriate for children. The authors tend to make the tenor less formal, and they often begin to personalise the text, including some of their own views. They also put in more descriptive adjectives. Less formal historical texts were identified by the use of personal references, with the author becoming more visible or known to the reader, for example, by putting in his/her own thoughts in their work.

Field words are used in these texts, but the authors also use words which in adult texts would not normally be associated with history. They use similes and metaphors, and allow the use of imagination and intuitive feelings, along with more descriptive adjectives and adverbs. Also some of the information would probably not be acceptable in formal historical texts, because it is based on guesswork rather than hard facts. Often the writer tries to get his/her readers to imagine what it would be like to live in certain historical situations.

> The long-haired soldiers of Greece stood on the plain. They faced the Trojans with murder in their hearts. The Greeks were as many and restless as the countless flies that swarm round cowsheds in spring.
> (The Greek and Roman World, Nicholl)

A comparison is given here but it is questionable if, to today's readers, it is useful to compare *flies around a cowshed* with *many soldiers*. How many children these days have seen a cowshed?

I found that many of the books had a historical type of register, especially at the beginning of books. Here is another example.

> The legionnaires were not at all impressed by the fact that the turbulent Britons were raiding the coasts of Gaul nor that the Britons' wealth in gold silver and lead would . . .
> They said they were quite comfortable where they were and saw no reason why they should fight. . . .
> (The story of Roman Britain, Baker)

There are more descriptive adjectives and adverbs in this extract than in the formal texts. Note the use of *turbulent, impressed.*

The use of *They said* is historical licence, because we have no evidence that this is what the legionnaires actually said.

Less formal Geographical

> An iceberg breaks from a glacier and moves into the sea. It is a large and glistening mountain of ice. It looks like a large castle. It is an island made of ice moving into the sea. Once this iceberg was part of a glacier. Icebergs break from glaciers that form in the far North and the far South.
> (Icebergs, Gans)

This is an interesting example because the author obviously thinks that she is making the text more accessible to children. The text is accompanied by both line drawings and 'pretty' drawings. All the same, I have found that children find this text very difficult to process and, because they have no idea what an iceberg is, they pick up on the words *castle* and *glistening* and think that the iceberg is a glistening castle.

Less formal Botanical/Natural

> The giraffe is the tallest animal in the world, gentle in behaviour and strangely beautiful. It has hoofs like an ordinary cow.
> (The Giraffe, Zebra Books)

This extract is from a book aimed at a very young audience. It is economical with words and uses much ellipsis (it should include *it is* gentle in behaviour and *it is* strangely beautiful), however the register is less formal. Books with heavy use of ellipsis are often difficult for children to understand, especially when they try reading them independently. Many of these books are probably designed for adults to read to children.

LESS FORMAL KEY GUIDE

> Tits are very pretty little birds and very friendly. Their sharp curved claws help them to cling to twig and string.
> (In your Garden, Ainsworth)

Compare this with the formal extract given as an example of the Identification Key Guide register. This text shows how key guides at the other end of the formality cline are written: they have longer sentences, little ellipsis, and adjectives and verbs are used normally.

BIOGRAPHICAL REGISTERS

The lexico-grammatical features of biographical writing have similarities with those of narrative works, probably because they are concentrating on life 'stories'. The extracts given here vary in the degree to which they follow the narrative format. However, these texts also have features in common with historical texts, for they are all written in the past tense and give a sense of history. They are often sequential and nearly always follow the course of just one person's life.

Some common field words and phrases are *little is known of*, *in ten years he had*, *in those early days there were*, and *at seventeen*. Mention of year dates and day dates are frequent. Authors often make judgements or evaluations in these texts.

This type of text may be more familiar to primary children than many of the previous types.

> In 1849 he made the most important decision of his life. He planned a long trip into the centre of Africa shooting, mapping and exploring in what was then almost unknown territory. To do this. . . .
> (Explorers of the Nile, Langley)

Here the author is setting the scene and explaining what conditions were like. It seems that in biographies, less prior knowledge is expected than in many subject registers. Often the texts elaborate on pure historical fact and biographers tend to romanticise their subject.

'LEARN AS YOU READ' REGISTER

Many adult texts are now written so readers can learn as they read. They are becoming more popular with the advent of Open Learning. There are now many distance learning colleges providing open learning texts, from the Open University to the Open College. The texts used are sometimes tailor-made for the courses, or are sometimes more general 'teach yourself' manuals. The formality or seriousness of the texts varies. The formality depends on the purpose of the text. For instance, it might be aimed at helping a reader to pass an exam or, at the other extreme, it might be encouraging the reader to learn for fun. Some of the books are based on 'programmed learning' and some give space for the reader to do an activity.

The children's texts also vary in these ways. The formality or tenor varied from text to text and some included more activities than others. Some texts were for very serious learning while others were suggestions for hobbies or outings. Nevertheless, they all gave some directions to their readers, who were often asked to carry out various activities. Some of the texts were more like exercise books, with more formalised activities requiring the children to make responses.

The extract below concerns hobbies or pursuits. It has an informal teacher-to-pupil tenor.

> There are several ways of studying trees. You can make collections of twigs and pressed leaves. You can press the flowers and collect dried fruits and seeds. And you can make brass rubbings.
> (Explorer's Guide – Trees, Chinery)

There is still to be found a type of text in the 'learn as you read' category of register that acts rather like an exercise book.

Exercise books

> The Romans in the picture are dressed as soldiers but everybody knows that it is not the dress that makes the man. The Romans had a definite idea of what one of their men should be like.
> Here is a list of Roman words. They are so much like English words that you can easily look them up in a dictionary if you do not know them already (many of our words today come from Latin, as the Roman language is called). These words describe the sort of qualities that a Roman was supposed to have.
> Fidelitas, fortitudo. . . .
> (The Romans and their Empire, Cairns)

This is a demanding text because the reader has to have much self-motivation to look up the words in a dictionary. It is more than likely that the writer expected this book to be used as a textbook with the teacher setting the tasks. *Everybody knows that it is not the dress that makes the man*: this statement is interesting, because the writer is either assuming that the reader will be familiar with the saying 'Manners maketh the man' or is expecting the teacher to explain it.

INSTRUCTIONAL REGISTERS

These registers are similar in many ways to the Learn as you Read texts, because readers must keep referring back to the text between other activities. The difference, however, is that these texts are not teaching the children new facts but explaining how to produce something, such as a model, a garment, a toy or a meal. Recipe text was a common example of the Instructional Register. A Do-It-Yourself manual would be an example of an adult text written in the instructional register.

With texts such as these, readers need to use a reading strategy different from that applied to other informational texts. They repeatedly read a small section, carry out a task and then return to the text to find out what to do next. To use this strategy one has to be able to scan text quickly to get back to the right place after each activity.

The features of these registers are heavy use of ellipsis, with few pronouns and usually very short, terse sentences. In recipes, the field words are cooking terms or technical words such as *sauté, heat, stir in, fold in, chop, slice*.

> Put the biscuits in a thick polythene bag. Hold the bag opening firmly together and crush the biscuits with a rolling pin. Measure very carefully into a saucepan.
> Level each. . . .
> (Easy Sweetmaking, Cox)

BEDSIDE BOOKS

Within the broad range of botanical books can be found a type of register that can be called the 'Bedside book'. This is a term often used by publishers. The example below is what I have described as a bedside book about the natural world.

> When people looked southwards from Europe towards Africa the first thing they saw was the desert. A vast expanse of sand and rock with no streams or rivers beginning on the southern slopes of the Mediterranean Sea. Europeans thought the desert was a world that could not be crossed . . .
> (Purnell's Animals of Europe)

The text jumps from one topic to another quite rapidly. It gives historical, geographical and biological information. Even so, the tenor is chatty. The author is trying not to impart knowledge but to give the reader the notion of what it might feel like to be in each country that is described. It is designed to be a relaxing read.

DIDACTIC TEXTS

The extracts that have been classified as didactic are not characterised by any single recognised subject area. What characterises them is their tenor. In each one the writer clearly wants readers to know something that they did not know before reading the book. Some writers obviously assume more prior knowledge in their readers than others, and although similar, the tenor is not uniform. In fact there is great variety in the formality of the texts. Some adopt a patronising tone towards the reader, while others suggest a more mature relationship.

This didactic type of text is prevalent in books for primary schools, in which the author is quite clearly trying to teach readers something new. The register is similar to that used in announcements for adults, such as BBC radio announcements giving warnings about dangers in the home. The writers of these announcements give straight facts with no embellishments. The following is an example of some straight didactic text.

> It is not true that brown eggs are any better than white ones. Eggs are one of our most popular foods. You can cook them in many ways.
> (Eggs, Hinds)

The next example is of informative didactic text.

> A Bedouin lives in the desert. He is travelling nearly all the time looking for fresh grazing ground for his animals. We call people who live like this nomads. Like a lot of other nomads the Bedouin lives in a tent because. . . .
> (The Book of the House, Carpi)

NARRATIVE

Continuing on the journey along the cline of formality, we come to some registers that are more likely to be found in children's information books than in adult texts. The first of these are the narrative registers.

The general differences between narrative and non-fiction texts have already been pointed out. The important point to remember is that narration is governed by story grammar.

An interesting fact about the narrative registers found in my study is that they are being used to convey information. The authors are clearly trying to impart knowledge, but their tenor is of a storyline nature. Some words and phrases are used in the text that would only very rarely be used in adult information texts, for instance *this is the story* or *suddenly*. Some of the extracts have cliff-hangers or suspense built into them, which again would not be found in an adult informative text. Some technical field words are used but, more frequently, the writer tries to avoid these and will try to choose easier synonyms instead.

The narrative registers are subdivided into three sub-categories on the cline of formality. These have been called didactic, false and real narrative.

The authors of these texts have probably chosen this type of register deliberately because they know that the expository register might be a problem for young children. The authors may think that the children will prefer this register, find it more interesting, easier to understand or perhaps easier to learn from. My feeling is that these books are in fact very confusing to the young reader and may be even more difficult to learn from, for the following reasons.

1   The books lack functional definition – are they fictional or factual? Children are expected to learn from these books, yet they are written in a story register.

2   Often the books have no structural guiders. Many of them have no headings, for example.

3   Children find it difficult with this type of text to distinguish fact from fiction.

4   The registers do not provide an adult model for children's writing.

Didactic Narrative

In this subdivision of narrative texts the authors try to tell a story at the same time as giving didactic information. They also include references to imaginary people. Readers cannot tell whether these people are real or fictional. Use is made of the personal reference *you*.

> They are very proud of this and Paulinus's ambition is to join the army. The infantry are called 'legionnaires'. They have to be Roman Citizens and above average height. There are 'auxiliaries' too who are troops of local soldiers with special skills, horsemen from Spain, archers from Syria, swimmers from Holland. Paulinus does not want to be an auxiliary he wants to be a legionary.
> (How They Lived in a Roman Fort, Thomas)

Here the story is told as though through the eyes of an imaginary soldier. Readers are not told in the book that this is an imaginary person. It is almost totally impossible to divorce fact from fiction unless one knows some background to the situation. It is as if the informative and narrative registers being combined to make a 'faction' register.

Faction is a common device in the modern media. Television companies, for instance, often produce documentaries in narrative form. The difference between the modern media programmes and the written texts in my study is that on television and radio the viewer is informed that the programme is 'faction' or 'docudrama' while the readers of the texts are not given this information.

False Narrative

> Patrice's father slit open the envelope containing his son's half term report, opened out the sheet of paper inside and began to read. Sitting opposite him at the breakfast table Patrice watched his father expectantly. '. . . hm . . . not bad . . .' grunted Herr Vetterli as he read through the list of marks. . . .
> When Monday dawned Patrice and his father set off for the observatory. . . . 'Dad tell me a bit about the observatory in general. . . .'
> (Time, Kurth)

This is another interesting extract because it demonstrates an approach that is often used in children's information books: that of the '*question* (from an unknowledgeable person) *and answer* (from knowledgeable person) *technique*'. The writer tries to recreate the oral register of an adult and child together, with the younger person constantly asking the older one questions.

Narrative

The texts in this group are genuine attempts at writing narrative. They follow the rules for a story grammar. The author tries to create a drama. They also use suspense and dialogue, with historical situations being personalised.

> "You must never ever say a word about our hiding places" warned the elder sister "Father Gerrard is called Mr Standish so that nobody will know he is a priest. And you must call him by that name. He would be in great danger and so would we if it were known. . ."
> (Hides and Seekers, National Trust)

This book continues to be like a story book throughout, even though it is advertised as an information book.

Another example would be:

> The story of wheat begins during Autumn, when grain is sown in the newly ploughed fields. Seeds which are safely covered will soon begin to germinate. Unburied seeds may be eaten by hungry birds.
> (The Cornfield, Luff)

This text actually uses the term *story*. The use of this word confuses many young readers, as they take the word literally. This particular book has also confused library ancillary staff as it has been classified as fiction in some schools.

Less Formal Biography

I include here an example of a less formal biography as there seems to be a certain type of biography that is on a very simplistic level.

> The castle is now up-to-date and newly whitewashed. Joan is Sir Guy's niece. While Sir Guy is often away from home serving the king Joan stays at Lidworth with his wife Lady Anne. Now twelve years old Joan has been. . . .
> (How they lived in a Medieval Castle, Adams)

This is a fascinating text because it seems typical of the texts that have been written especially to make the knowledge more accessible to young children. However the text produces anomalies. It is historical and tries to impart knowledge but is written in the present tense. It is written in a biographical manner but the characters are presumably fictitious.

CHILDREN'S ANOMALOUS REGISTERS

Erratic Register

There are several children's informational texts that change register so often that this erratic quality is, in fact, the register. The extracts given in this category all include changes of register in mid-flow. As already pointed out, registers are expected to change over the course of a text but not so abruptly as these do. The extracts suggest that the books have a confused function: they do not seem to be either informational or narrative. This type of erratic register is very unusual in adult texts.

One of the best examples of a text changing registers in mid-flow is the one below. The double oblique lines show where the register changes abruptly.

> It's raining. On go our raincoats and up go the umbrellas. // Mind those puddles. // Water has more than one form. It is always in the air as water vapour. // Even though you cannot see it. . . . It has been raining for days. // As water runs into the river its level rises. Finally the river bursts its banks.
> (Water, Leutscher)

Consider the change of register between *Mind those puddles* and *Water has more than one form*. The first sentence is talking about a picture in the book, which is followed immediately by a sentence in a scientific register stating a fact, and using field words (*form*). The second section changes just as quickly: *It has been raining for days. As water runs into the river its level rises.*

Implicit references to illustrations

It seems that one of the characteristics of children's information books is the frequent reference to the illustrations. In some books there are no captions and so the authors make references to the illustrations from within the text. These texts have implicit references to the illustrations.

Readers of these books are guided to the illustrations by use of demonstrative references. *This* is used frequently, as in *there are restaurants like this in America/this is a banquet*. Also the demonstrative *the* is often used as in *the bee comes to the dandelion*. Another way in which the writer guides the reader to the illustration is by using the pronominal *you* and using words synonymous with look e.g. *see*.

Often texts in this register make references to imaginary people. They also tend to make use of ellipsis. The present tense is used in all of them. This helps the reader identify with the pictures because they seem concrete as opposed to abstract.

It should be noted that these texts require children to cope with additional reading skills, because they have to lift their eyes from the text and then find their correct place again. This may not be that difficult a task but it is an extra one. A survey of adult texts suggests that such features are not often found in adult books.

Here are some examples.

> The squirrel will save the mushroom for winter when there isn't any other food around. Can you see the acorns it has also collected? This big mushroom is fully grown. The gills are brown. When it rains other mushrooms pop up from the earth.
> (The Mushroom, Ingves)

This extract demonstrates the use of *the* instead of *a*. Objects, in this case the squirrel and the mushroom, are given a pretend identity.

> Look at this picture what do you see?
> But that soil was dry and bare. To cover it with grass we would need seeds like these. How many seeds do you think there are in this little pile? The seeds will need food from the soil. How many bags of fertilizer can you see in this picture? What does fertilizer do? . . . if you opened the case of this vegetable what seeds would you find? This is an apple tree in flower. The tree flowers in spring. The apples grow throughout the summer.
> (Things That Grow, Pluckrose)

This extract is meaningless without the photographs. It makes use of the pictures in the most direct way.

Questions

These texts cannot really be regarded as having a distinct register, but there is certainly a type of children's text that includes many unanswered questions. This is not helpful in developing the children's research skills because unless the texts suggest where to look up information the readers cannot learn from them.

The following extract relies very heavily on questions. The book appears to be intended to be read aloud by an adult or a child. When adults read books like this aloud, they tend not to use the text provided but simply to use the illustrations as talking points.

> Tell me the time. It's 7 o'clock.
> Time to wake up. Get out of bed and get washed.
> Can you get dressed by yourself?
> Tell me the time. It's 8 o'clock. Time for breakfast.
> You could have cornflakes or eggs or toast or fruit?
> What do you like to eat for breakfast?
> (Tell Me The Time, Bradbury)

CONCLUSION

These findings show that, even in books on one topic, children are expected to be able to cope with a vast array of registers. In any one day, children might experience many of these registers in their reading. Many teachers have probably never realised that children have to face this range of registers every day of their primary years.

Some of the demands of the English National Curriculum were quoted on pages 39 and 77–8. Even so, it is pertinent to point out here two further stipulations. At Key Stage 1 the Programmes of Study demand that:

> teachers should cover a range of rich and stimulating texts both fiction and non-fiction.

At Key Stage 2:

> pupils should hear good non-fiction read aloud.

Children find writing in an informative register very difficult. (More is written about this in Chapters 7 and 8.) One of the reasons for this is that they do not hear enough of how the language should sound. This is why the English committee on the National Curriculum is suggesting that teachers should read aloud informative texts. The problem is that there are so few good quality or 'rich and stimulating' books to choose from.

I hope that the two demands quoted above, together with the last three chapters of this book, will encourage teachers to look more closely at the informative texts on their shelves and to consider how many books can really be classed as rich and stimulating. How many of them will hold your children's attention?

7 How can children's information books be made more usable?

This chapter discusses the following questions, which arise from the findings in Chapter 6.

1 What is the value of specialist language to children?

2 What is the value of anomalous registers to children?

3 What is the relationship between readability and register?

SPECIALIST REGISTERS

A number of specialist registers were found in the children's books. It is interesting to speculate whether this type of register is helpful or unhelpful to young children's reading for learning.

Many educationalists think that subject texts are frequently full of jargon, and some will go so far as to state that this jargon is used as a 'membership qualification': if you cannot understand the language, you are not a member. Quadling (1981) called it 'A conspiracy of difficulty'. Certainly my research and the work of others suggests that specialist registers can be a problem to young readers.

Science has been found to be the most challenging register (Graham, 1978; Lunzer and Gardner, 1979) followed by Mathematics (Watkins, 1979; Rothery, 1986). The work of Watkins and of Rothery suggests that the reading skills required for mathematics must be explicitly taught. History has been found to present difficulties too (Wishart, 1986; Harold Rosen in Cashdan and Grugeon, 1972). The latter study points out that any history book will contain sentences such as *monasteries had formed part of English life*. Superfically this may seem simple but, as Rosen points out, children have to ask themselves questions like 'What does this really mean?' 'What is a monastery?' 'How does it form part of English life?' 'What is English life?' This highlights again the importance of prior knowledge for comprehension.

The alternative school of thought about the usefulness of specialist language is made up mainly of academics and specialists. They believe that specialised technical language is useful to the reader, for without specialist language and technical terms a subject would lose its definition and identity. Subject academics are often so familiar with the formal registers of their discipline that they cannot see how these could be inhibiting to less experienced readers.

Gillham (1986) makes the following plea to specialists:

> As professional communicators we must try to:
> *Ensure* that our subject is delivered in a context likely to enhance comprehension . . .
> We must all come to terms with the fact that we are normally not teaching children who will become specialists in our own field.
> (Gillham, 1986)

However, it seems that in reality the educationalists and academics are often not so far apart as has been suggested. Educationalists are beginning to appreciate that children have to be initiated into specialist registers, with each subject teacher playing his or her part in this task. At the same time, educationalists and teachers are calling for the amount of specialist language in many texts to be reduced. If these two trends continue, we will arrive at a situation in which young children, who are not after all going to become experts in every field, will be able to read with understanding without being handicapped (Calfee and Curley, 1984; Gillham, 1986).

It must be remembered that some subjects do have a specialist layout and a way of approaching the subject which should not be totally lost. One text type that has evolved over centuries, and which children may find difficult to understand, is that of zoology. Zoologists always use the same basic outline to describe various types of animals (appearance, habitat, etc.), so this text type has become an accepted feature of their subject. Another example is the register that was found quite clearly in this study – the Identification Key Guide. Though this register can be very formal, there were also some quite acceptable texts based on it which made reasonably easy reading for the amateur botanist.

Perera (1981) divides technical vocabulary into two types. The first type consists of words that are necessary and helpful because they encapsulate key concepts which non-technical words would be too imprecise to express neatly or effectively. The second type consists of jargon: these words are not essential as they just make the text more difficult. The dichotomy of useful versus unhelpful language is evident in children's topic books.

> The explanations offered in children's texts are necessarily simplified forms of more complex explanations. Consequently pressure is on the author of children's texts to use short simple sentences, easy vocabulary words, omit less important details or procedures and condense the explanation of many ideas into a relatively small number of words.
>
> (Anderson, Armbruster and Kantor, 1980)

ANOMALOUS REGISTERS

There is a group of texts that has been identified in my study as 'Anomalous'. It has been assumed that these texts represent attempts by authors and publishers to overcome the specialist formal register problem. Very often the books pretend to the reader that they are story texts, when in fact they are aiming to impart knowledge. I suggest, on the basis of my work with children, that the attempts may not always be successful. These registers are artificial, and often have no equivalent adult register. They often seem to create their own problems.

In the first place it is important to remember that these Anomalous texts have become widely accepted as a useful part of our children's literature. The Macdonald Junior Reference books are one of the most popular series in schools (Baum and Ingham, 1983). In more academic circles, Chapman and Louw have suggested that:

> Educationally these texts have sound stratagems of moving pupils from the familiar register of narrative fiction, which is reading for pleasure, towards registers of history and geography which are read for acquisition of facts and the development of concepts.
>
> (Chapman and Louw, 1986)

However, the same authors go on to point out that there is a limit to how useful a narrative style might be. For instance, a maths text would not start off with:

> Once upon a time there was this little algebraic equation. It lived in a far off palace and its family was made up of x's and y's. . . .
>
> (Chapman and Louw 1986)

This text might sound ridiculous but some of the texts which have been quoted in this study are equally bizarre.

Another finding of my study was that many of the books with anomalous registers are banal and have nothing of interest for the reader to absorb. Very often the information is so basic that children already know the facts before reading the text. This is in complete contrast to the texts that have been identified as having a 'concept overload'. The Anomalous texts fall into two classes: one class of texts say nothing that the children do not know already, and the other class give so much information in such a small number of words that children cannot absorb the new data. In these books, the text has no redundancy – nothing to throw away.

Morgens Jansen is heavily critical of our children's information books. He has noted that in Danish, as well as the terms *narrative* and *expository* there is a third term which we do not have in English. This term means:

> A non-fiction [book] the presentation of which is mainly sustained by
> 'fiction elements': the well told non-fiction which has fiction over-
> tones, *but is* [his italics] non-fictional – and absolutely correct.
> (Jansen, 1987, written in English)

Jansen suggests that this type of literature equates to the new journalism or the dramatised documentary, the so-called docudrama. He suggests that it is a hybrid between fact and fiction. It is interesting to note that the Thai language also has a word for this type of book.

Jansen suggests that in Britain we are holding our youngsters back because we treat them as immature. He postulates that it is impossible to publish a book for 8 year-olds in Denmark which is non-fiction but pretends to be fictional. He states that the Danish children just would not accept such a book because they would realise it was not useful: they demand that books should be factually correct. It is suggested that our publishers ought to take note of this, and to treat our youngsters in a more adult manner.

Another problem that was highlighted in my study and is pursued in Chapter 8 is that created by familiar words being used in a specialist way. Often children get confused by a word having more than one meaning. They latch on to the more familiar meaning and lose sense of a whole section of text. This is supported by the work of Perera (1981). I have found through discussions with various groups of teachers that instructors of the deaf are well aware of this problem because sign language has to explain the meaning of these words.

Another aspect of the anomalous registers which seems problematic for children is that of cohesion. Cohesion is best explained as a linking system. The reason that a text is a text rather than a series of disconnected sentences is that within their texts authors create links, often by use of connectives. Connectives link two sentences or parts of a sentence together. It was shown that the connectives used in informative texts differ from those used in narrative's. Some simplistic or anomalous texts try not to use them at all.

Many of the anomalous books use devices such as implicit references to the illustrations. Irwin (1983) undertook one of the few studies on this subject and she found that explicit references were easier to understand than implicit ones. Her work supports my suggestion in this book that implicit references to illustrations are probably more difficult to cope with than captions, and also make the task less like adult reading.

Another type of text that was identified in my study was that which includes many unanswered questions. In my experience, the fact that these texts have so many questions often makes the child want to reject the text rather than find out the answers. Tierney, Mosenthal and Kantor also feel strongly about this type of text:

> Simple basal narratives are often sabotaged by an excessive use of trivial questioning.
> (Tierney, Mosenthal and Kantor, 1984)

I have rarely come across a child who is inspired to go and find out the answer to any of these questions, probably because no advice is given as to how to find the answers. Also, the questions seem to direct the child, and therefore fail to foster the child's natural curiosity.

It seems that ellipsis is more common in information books than in narratives, and it makes them harder to understand. The anomalous texts in this study were often marked by heavy use of ellipsis. It seems that writers are using ellipsis to keep the readability level down, because it is one way of keeping the sentences short.

READABILITY AND REGISTER

In Chapter 4 it was shown that many books intended for children have a high readability level if assessed using readability formulae. Many others have a falsely lowered readability level, that is they have been written to achieve a low score when assessed by formulae. Neither of these type of texts are helpful to children.

It was also suggested that one of the major problems of applying readability formulae to information books is that they do not take into account the varying amount of prior knowledge each reader has. The fact that a reader is highly knowledgeable about a particular subject will often make a text on that subject very readable for that individual. The same can be said in reverse – readers who have very limited background knowledge on a subject, however good they are at reading, will always have difficulties with texts in that subject. In schools, children start on new projects at least once a term. At the start of each project they have little background knowledge and thus the texts are likely to seem difficult for them.

It has been suggested that reading any informative text is more difficult for young children than reading a narrative text. However, it has also been suggested that producing books that are written to readability formulae does not necessarily make the text any easier to read.

In the words of Perera:

> children's books should not be written in the simplest language for, if they are, pupils would lose a very valuable means of extending their reading and language abilities.
> (Perera, 1981)

INFORMATION BOOKS – THE CINDERELLA OF TEXTS?

It has been argued in the first part of this book that information and retrieval skills are essential and that children must know how to manipulate information, how to make sense of it, and how to make it work for them. Literacy demands are becoming greater all the time and it is my view that reading for information must start in the primary school. Informative reading is now a major part of the English National Curriculum. At present, though, the information books that are provided for primary aged children are, on the whole, inadequate. They also provide children with a very poor model of adult information books. In many cases the children are either offered a banal, insipid version that lacks function, organisation and sufficient challenge, or a demanding specialised version which lacks the characteristics of language with which young children are familiar.

The findings of my study suggest that the books are more diverse than they are similar. Consequently children have no consistent group of texts from which to learn the skills of informative reading: there seems to be no norm for the children's informative book. They vary enormously in length, they vary in function, they vary in readability, they vary in depth of topic, they vary in register, they vary in the amount of specialist language used, they vary in their expectations of the pupil and they also vary in their inspiration and the commitment of their authors. Very often they appear to be a type of text that has no equivalent adult model.

Young children are probably the last group of readers who should be given such a wide variety of texts. They need a model from which to learn, and with which to become familiar. They also need a good model for their own writing since children learn by modelling their work on that which is provided for them. Teachers should not have to present primary children with second-best texts or re-issued adult books. Ideally they should be given a model that excels, a model that they will immediately recognise as an informative book. The book should inspire and interest young readers. Their structure should be sound and the organisation should enable readers to find their way around the texts with ease.

Many higher educational establishments, such as the Open University and the Open College, are now employing open learning techniques. Even if children are not learning completely by open learning techniques in the primary school, they will be expected to use them more and more as they move up the educational ladder. Only with a good model of an informative book will teachers be able to help children to read in a reflective manner and to enable them to search out the meaning behind the words.

One of the reasons for our problems with information books in this country is that so little interest is taken in informative texts. It is time that far more emphasis was put on research into informative texts, as opposed to narrative. As Williams (1983) has urged:

> If a fraction of the research effort, time and money currently spent, directly or indirectly, on teaching pupils to read content-field textbooks were to be diverted to helping authors to write more readable textbooks, then many of the pupil's problems would be eased.
> (Williams, 1983)

Unless the teaching profession demands better quality books, publishers will probably not make the necessary changes. Some money also ought to be made available for materials to be trialled with different aged children, for we can all suggest that the texts are deficient in some way, but no adult really knows how clearly children understand these texts. Research in this area would be of immense value. There ought to be a collaborative team of reading experts working together with publishers. Publishers often do not know enough about reading psychology and the greatest failing of these books is that they lack practical evidence of what has been leant from psychology or learning theories. We have to put learning theories to work in these books. It must be stressed that any future research must be based in the classroom to enable the researcher to work closely with groups of children.

As a result of the findings from this study, it seems appropriate to call these books the Cinderella of books.

To improve the present situation it is suggested that publishers should keep to simpler topics and not try to simplify more abstract and difficult ones. Secondly, they should encourage their writers to write on a more limited subject in greater depth than is done at present. For instance, instead of producing another book on Ourselves which is a very popular topic, they should produce a series of books on particular aspects of the body such as Ears, Hands, Feet, Circulation, or The Family which might include Babies, Toddlers and Brothers or Sisters. At present many of the books just whet the child's appetite and do not allow him or her to satiate his or her hunger by providing enough depth of topic.

The fundamental aim of children's books should be to create a dialogue between writer and reader. Obviously, it is very difficult for writers to judge how much prior knowledge their readers will have and they will never get the balance right for all of their readers. Readers are always going to vary in their background knowledge and experiences. However, this does not mean that writers for the junior audience could not make more suitable assumptions about the young children's prior knowledge than they often do in the books highlighted in this study.

It might be safer to explain everything and assume the child has no background knowledge of the subject. Often, in these books, it was the really basic concepts that authors assumed the readers would know.

I know that it is not easy to write informative texts. As Wright (1987) has stated 'It is easy to criticise. And it is very hard to do well'. He continues to explain the problems:

> The books need to be simple in language and simple (but not simplistic) in content, in concepts and in choice of themes. . . . If you are brief, you are not so likely to be interesting: the interesting topic has to stop just after it starts. If you are accurate you probably have lots of use for "usually", "often", "in general" – and there's no better way of killing interest and enjoyable reading.
> (Wright, 1987)

This is all very true but there is no excuse for the standard of writing being as low as it is with some examples of text not even making sense.

Jansen (1987) has put the difficulties of writing informative texts in verse:

> It is easy
> to write difficult,
> and it is difficult
> to write easy.

It is difficult
to write easy
for ordinary readers
about difficult concepts.

And it is extremely difficult
to write very easy
for weaker readers
about difficult concepts.
(Jansen, 1987, written in English)

As was suggested in an earlier chapter, there are two views on who should do the writing. One view is that experts in the field ought to do the writing and the other is that reading experts ought to be responsible for the language and layout of the books. I seriously suggest that the best solution is for experts and reading specialists to work more co-operatively. One could help the other.

However suggesting that more new books should be written does not imply that teachers should not continue to select appropriate books. The selection process is still very important. Anderson and Armbruster (1984) have equated the selection of books with buying a pair of shoes. First teachers found out the child's reading age and then matched it to a certain readability. It is suggested that in future we should not put so much emphasis on matching the reader and text but look more at books that will provide the reader with "learnability" factors. Which books are more likely to provide a good model for learning? We should compare the selecting process with that of choosing a computer. Hence asking questions such as: Which one is sufficient to my needs? Which one can I use quickly? Is the book user friendly?

USABILITY

The term *usability* was coined by Orna and it seems to me that this is a very suitable term that could be applied to children's informative books. Orna (1985) offers this definition of usability:

A usable text is one that allows a successful transaction to take place between user and maker.
(Orna 1985)

In this transaction the user's (or reader's) initial unsatisfactory state of knowledge (which is what makes him or her a user in the first place) is transformed, by gaining access to knowledge that the maker (or writer) has structured to meet the user's needs. As a result of reading the usable text, the user becomes master of new information. It is this emphasis on children being able to find out for themselves that makes the term usability attractive.

At present the author suggests that the standard guidelines for the selection of books should be:

Can I, as an adult, find my way around this book?

Can I easily make sense of it?

Does the book interest me?

and the crucial question is:

Can I learn new information from this book?

In conclusion I think that, at present, a great deal of money is being spent inappropriately by schools. Information books often lie dormant on library shelves or are only browsed through. As to being used for study, this is an illusion. What very often appears to be study is not – it might be a general survey to get the best pictures to illustrate a topic or alternatively the text is read with a passive approach which is unlikely to produce any real learning. Sometimes the student may not have the right reading skills to cope with a serious expository text but very often the books fail to give satisfaction to serious young students of learning.

My hope is that this book will raise the interest level of educationalists, researchers and publishers of children's informative books and consequently, to produce a bank of research that will be of practical value, based on the question: how can we write expository books for young children that will make them usable by children and allow these youngsters real opportunities to learn from texts?

A list of recommendations concerning the format of the books will now be made. These are for a set of books which will be excellent examples of texts from which the children would be able to find out for themselves.

RECOMMENDATIONS

1   Authors should be chosen with care. They should either be experts in their own field or reading experts. The former group of authors should be people who care and understand that the books they produce will be read by children who may not have the same love of the subject or the same understanding of its accompanying specialised language as themselves. The second group of authors should be

reading experts who themselves research into the subject in hand, write the draft text, and then collaborate with an expert in the field to produce the final version.

2 Authors and publishers should choose their topic focus with great care. They should also give considerable thought to the depth of the topic. They should ask questions such as: How much do we want the reader to know about the subject? Is there anything new for the reader in the book? Is there too much new knowledge in the book? Are there anchor points with existing knowledge?

Authors must write with their audience in mind and be aware of just how much basic knowledge some readers will require. Texts should try to seek out and develop existing concepts, thus making information as predictable and accessible as possible.

3 The layout of the pages must be clear. It must be obvious which parts of the text one is expected to read first. The book should have page numbers for easy reference.

4 The book should have a logical structure. A book, from which one is to learn, ought to have:

- An advance organiser – stating what the reader will be reading, why, and what he/she will know at the end of the read. If the book does not have an advance organiser, it should have a well-written introduction which is easily read by the intended audience. The introduction should be easily identified.

- There should be a summary at the end of the book and possibly one at the end of each chapter, picking out the facts or concepts which the author assumes are new to the reader. The summaries could then be a model for the students' own reviews.

- A title which reviews the whole text would be helpful.

- The book should have well-chosen sub-headings. The text below the heading should be relevant to that heading. The number of words to a heading and in a caption must be related to the ability of the expected audience. No real advice can be given on the number of words under each heading, however, it is likely that somewhere between 75 and 300 words would be appropriate.

- Contents pages should be well laid out in language that is no more difficult than the rest of the book. The contents page should be uncluttered and should give the reader a quick preview of the author's layout and the subject of the book.

- Books should have interesting illustrations with well-sited captions preferably in a typeface which is different from that of the main text.

- Books should have an index, with perhaps some clues on its use. Only proper references should be included with no references just to the mention of a word.

- Books should have 'a blurb' on the back cover. It should give the reader a general overview of the book. It should not be any harder to read than the main text.

5 Other features of some books that might not be appropriate in many project titles would be:

- Glossaries which are readable and understandable. These should not be written in terms of other new concepts. Some topics will benefit from glossaries more than others.

- Bibliographies should be included. Annotated bibliographies are especially useful. Acknowledgments should also be included if at all possible.

6 The books must be functionally informative. This must be reflected in their layout and the register of the language used. Books should not have dual functions. They should be written in a register that suggests the text is enabling the reader to learn. In terms of the analysis in Chapter 5 probably the register should be semi-informal subject register or a didactic/informative register. Unnecessary technical vocabulary should be avoided though specialised language should be used rather than simplistic synonyms. Text should be written in clear sentences which should not be unnecessarily long. The texts should have cohesion and use connectives in a natural way.

7 The author should use metadiscourse to advantage. This is where the author makes him/herself known and 'visible' to the reader through the use of the personal voice. The author should use signposts such as 'we will do this and then we will do this'.

The texts should be interesting and encouraging to the reader.

8 Authors should bear in mind the term usability when writing rather than concentrating on the term readability.

9 The text should be accurate. If there is more than one opinion on a topic this should be clearly stated. (There is the whole area of research into the possibility of books being racially and sexually unbiased but this is too large an area to discuss here.)

10 The size and type of print should be appropriate to the age group.

The ultimate test when selecting an information book, whether it is aimed at a child or not, should be: Do I enjoy this book? Can I learn from it? Can I find the answers to my questions?

8 How to teach children to use information books

I have written at length about the failings of the books presently in our school libraries and bookshops. This does not mean that I wish to discourage teachers from using these books in the classroom. I hope that this chapter will encourage more teachers to use information books in a constructive manner, as there are several useful strategies that can be used on these books despite their drawbacks.

This chapter includes activities which I hope will help you to understand the process of active reading.

NOTEMAKING

Activity 1

Were you ever taught how to use an information book?
Were you ever taught notemaking at school?

I expect that for most people the answer to both questions is 'no'. I have found that few adults have ever been taught how to retrieve information. Those who have been taught often feel that their skills in this area are inadequate or ineffective.

The most famous piece of research on student notemaking was carried out in 1959 by Perry. He described how many Harvard students exhibited 'obedient purposelessness' when asked to read a complex chapter. Later research clearly suggested that if study skills are taught at sixth form level or university they make little real impact on the student (Gibbs, Morgan and Taylor, 1980). This is because the students have been using inappropriate strategies for too long and find it very difficult to change.

Activity 2

Are you good at making notes?
Are you confident of retrieving the right information?

Again in my experience most adults do not see themselves as good notemakers, and do not feel confident that they can retrieve the right information from a book. I have found that those who do have the expertise are those that have learned 'on the job'. They have usually been required to carry out a great deal of reading, and because of these demands, they have had to change their reading strategies. Research quoted in Chapter 1 lead us to the conclusion that notemaking is being neither constructively or consistently taught in primary schools. It is to be hoped that this will change with the advent of the National Curriculum.

One problem with notemaking is that class teachers do not appreciate how much practice is required for children to become effective note-makers. Moreover, the very children who need the most help in this regard are probably the ones who get the least practice at it. Campione and Armbruster (1985) found that weak readers in the States were given less practice and instruction than good readers in the use of a variety of notemaking strategies.

Activity 3

What problems do you have with notemaking?

In answer to this question, most adults and youngsters will cite similar difficulties. The problems most often quoted are as follows.

1 Making text redundant: poor notemakers lack confidence in their ability to select the right words, so they usually want to write the text out verbatim.

2 Putting the text into one's own words: most poor notemakers have difficulty getting away from copying. They have difficulty with finding their own words and feel that the author has always chosen the best ones.

3 Reorganisation of text: most poor notemakers find it very difficult to get away from the original text structure – this problem leads to more severe difficulties if more than one book is being consulted.

Activity 4

Which notemaking strategies have you developed?
You may not have been taught notemaking but you have probably developed some sort of strategy: what is it?

Adults use a great variety of strategies but very often each individual only has perhaps two or at best three different ways of making notes. Most adults, however, will admit to some form of text marking. It might take the form of underlining, highlighting or placing double lines beside paragraphs. This is especially true now photocopying is relatively cheap and there are so many types of highlighter pen readily available.

A large number of adults also admit to some form of copying – not usually word for word but not far from this. Some leave out the odd sentence, the odd word, or make abbreviations. The variety of strategies is enormous, and many individuals, have devised their systems gradually over the years. It is suggested by research on adults (Gibbs, Morgan and Taylor, 1980) that notemaking is an individualistic activity: a strategy may work for one person but not for another. It is also suggested by Gibbs (1981) that adults should be taught a variety of skills so that they can select the one that is best for them. Having a number of skills from which to select is probably important for children as well.

Notemaking is a demanding activity. To be effective it must involve the reader in thinking. However, I need to stress that children must first be taught how informative text differs from narrative, and they must be taught to become flexible active readers.

ACTIVE READING

Chapter 1 discussed the importance of active reading and showed that children are often insufficiently challenged by particular texts. Very often they have been taught to read so that they can absorb a story but very little else. To read about a subject that is new, and that one knows little about, is challenging. One's mind must be actively searching through the text for the information one seeks, interacting with and questioning the text.

Activity 5

Read the newspaper extract shown in figure 8.1 overleaf.
Now read the same text with the aim of finding out the chief executive's view of the current interest rates and why Trafalgar House profits have been cut by half.

It is difficult here to make this task realistic. However, in the first task when I just asked you to read the passage and gave you no purpose, you may have switched off. You would not have known which parts of the text were more important than others, and may not even have been motivated to read the

Trafalgar House profits cut in half

Tony May

THE severity of the UK recession has more than halved the mid-year profits of the Trafalgar House group to £51.5 million and there is little sign of an improvement in the second half.

The chairman, Sir Nigel Broackes, said the serious downturn in the UK and US had hit most sectors of the property and housing business. In addition, the Gulf war lopped £15 million off profits of the shipping and hotel divisions as nervous customers postponed cruises and trips to Europe. This business is picking up, but slowly.

The heavy engineering and construction businesses had a record year and margins are up from 3 per cent to 3.3 per cent. The construction order book is a record £2.9 billion.

The chief executive, Sir Eric Parker, said: "We anticipate a rotten 1991." But on the basis of the potential recovery in 1992, he saw no reason to cut the in-terim dividend which is held at 8.8p a share.

He called for a cut in interest rates to get industry going, but does not look for a quick recovery in the economy.

The housebuilding business sold 900 houses in the UK in the first half and 170 overseas. That compared with 1,150 and 210 in the previous year, but Sir Eric expected to see 2,300 in the UK and 500 overseas by the year end. Margins were still under pressure, but the underlying demand was good with first-time buyers expected to come into the market strongly after the next interest rate cut.

The group would like to take advantage of the weakness of its rivals in the construction industry by making acquisitions on a world-wide basis, but Sir Eric thinks asking prices are too high.

The commercial property market in the UK has become so weak that rather than sell its £200 million of property developments off at knock-down prices, the board has decided to keep them as investments.

Fig. 8.1   Cutting from the *Guardian*, May 9 1991

text at all. If you bothered to make notes, you would probably have made jottings on what interested you or what you saw as the most important.

The second task should have made your mind much more alert. You were told to search within the text for particular facts. Having a question in mind makes readers active: they interact with the text, knowing what to look for, distinguishing what is important from what is not.

So rule number one is to be an active reader. It is obviously crucial that children are encouraged to make their reading active, to read with questions in their minds. All too often teachers give children reading tasks but do not tell them why they are reading or what to look for. This encourages passive reading. In one of the few studies on young children using notemaking, Taylor (1986) found that children were unable 'to read for an audience other than themselves'. Rather than selecting the most important idea for a general audience from the text, several of the children had the confused notion that the most unusual or unfamiliar ideas should be picked out. For instance, the children thought that a summary ought to contain what the audience would like to know and not just the important ideas in the text. Taylor found, as I have done, that children's selection of key words was based on what interested them or what they thought their peers would enjoy. As Campione and Armbruster wrote:

> It seems that for poor readers, importance may be based on factors which captured their interest.
> (Campione and Armbruster, 1985)

FINDING THE MAIN IDEA

Much of the work in notemaking consists of finding the main idea in a piece of text. Some methodology books which teach children notemaking emphasise this concept, but as Taylor's work showed, children do not necessarily know how to select the main idea in a text.

The ability to select the main idea or gist of a passage has in the past been subject to a fair amount of scientific investigation. Few pieces of research concentrated on primary aged children, however. Otto and White (1982) asked children aged between 6 and 12 years to read a paragraph and to make up just one sentence in their own words that would combine what all the sentences said. None of the children were good at this task, although it was found that they did improve with age. Other research suggests that young children can give the main idea if the passage has a simple structure, but not otherwise. Texts that have a simple structure are very often found in books that have been specially written for exercises that promote 'main idea' work but, in my view, this simplistic structure is rarely found in normal texts. Pearson and Johnson said:

> We know of no aspect of comprehension so universally accepted yet so often confused as the notion of "finding the main idea".
> (Pearson and Johnson, 1978)

I have certainly found the activity of trying to find key words unhelpful for young children. They need to be set a specific reading task. Children cannot identify what is important in a text if they do not know what to look for. Children often think a particular piece of information is of significance if it interests them, while the teacher may well think it is insignificant. For instance, I have had children pick up the term 'cousins' in a text on animal classification. The author did not mean the term to be important, but it was concrete for the children and they could relate to it. In a way these children were right: they spotted what they did not know.

Activity 6

Read the article in figure 8.2 opposite. Underline in green those words that tell you if standards have fallen. Underline in blue those words that tell you what affects children's reading. Underline in red those words that tell you why information reading is different from fiction reading.

You will notice that you have underlined different parts of the text. There is no one set of key words: it depends on your purpose. If you have no purpose then all of the text (or none of it) becomes important. It is the same for children. If they have not set themselves a specific purpose for reading, they think that the whole book is important: they are not selective, and this leads to copying.

So rule number two is to be a purposeful reader. Children's reading must be purposeful they must have questions in their mind before they do any reading. One of the demands of the national curriculum is that children be able to read to answer their own pre-set questions. However, the crux of the problem is *how do you get children to ask good questions?* This is of vital importance because all good research is based on good questions. Unless the questions are relevant then the research has no meaning.

When children first try to create questions they think of those to which they already know the answers, or they think of questions that are so unrealistic that nobody would ever be able to find the answer to them. It is therefore important that children are taught to devise good quality questions.

Teaching children to devise questions

This is how I help children to think of good questions. First I teach the children to brainstorm. They produce a mass of words that are connected with their project. Having collected them into thought units they put them on different coloured branch lines as shown in figure 8.3 overleaf. When they can think of no more words to go on to the ends of the branch lines then that is the extent of their knowledge. They do not know anything else about that subject.

The children are then asked to select a word at the end of one of the branch lines, and to select one of the following question words:

Page 20, November 13, 1990

Fact and reading fiction

Michael Marland's CURRICULUM COUNSEL

THE notion that reading is one of the most important keys to educational success is agreed by all: newspaper critics, devoted teachers and parents. But what is happening to standards? Employers are critical: "It is a great surprise and disappointment to us to find that our young employees are so hopelessly deficient in their command of English." Many may long for the golden days, but that quotation *was* from those days — Lever Brothers Ltd reporting to the Newbolt Report in 1921. The complaints of today are remarkably like those of the past.

The latest panic was prompted by a very limited study by a group of educational psychologists using a dubious test. No wonder that Brian Cox, chair of the National Curriculum Working Party for English, castigated it for intellectual sloppiness. Yet there are detailed research studies that illuminate reading problems. In May the University of Surrey showed that the more lead, aluminium or zinc in a child's body as tested by hair or saliva tests, the lower the reading scores. Did that get widely reported?

In Leicester research focused on left- and right-handedness. Fascinatingly, the researchers found that there is a connection between reading and skill with the left or right hands: children with either a very strong right- or very strong left-hand skill are likely to have poorer reading skills. Did that get widely reported?

The same fears are repeated often: "But are they being taught to read?" The worries appear to be misdirected. Yes, there are serious doubts about whether the present curriculum is helping effective reading, but it is not the early stages that are weak. Nor is it, contrary to much printed panic, because of too little teaching of phonics. It is because we stop developing reading skills except in the teaching of literature. We are extraordinarily good at teaching fiction. Reading for learning is something different but equally

important. This is how we grapple with ideas, arguments and the discourse of GCSE and Higher Education.

Fiction, marvellous as it is as an art form, is a poor training for the reading of non-narrative. The story carries the reader along and stimulates the understanding of the text without too much conscious effort. When those pupil-readers hit a text explaining facts or arguments, they expect the same thing to work and are disappointed and baffled when it does not.

This is partly due to sentence length and structure: the average sentence in fiction (according to one US computer analysis) is as low as 11 words, whereas in learned and scientific writing sentences average 21 words. They are often of a different structure to those in stories, with far more subordinate clauses. The paragraphs are also different: fiction keeps rolling. Non-fiction writing has ideas followed by arguments, followed by examples, before returning to a second argument. Seeing the structure of a non-narrative paragraph is to see the pattern of the argument and reading fiction will not help a pupil develop this skill.

The words used are equally different. In the articulation of argument

"signal words" are very important: *however, despite, accordingly, although, since, while.* Those last two confuse pupils. They have met them mostly as words concerned with time. In non-narrative, however, they demonstrate the argument. These words are the untaught words of the curriculum.

The key conceptual words are often derived from Latin or Greek, and our curriculum rarely gives access to even a modest understanding of their meanings and stress patterns. Science and medicine inhabit a world-wide *constructed* vocabulary, derived from the ancient western world. The relationship between the spelling of words like "haematology" and how young people come to pronounce them requires further study.

What is certain is that our pupils will not have access to higher education without specific reading tuition in non-narrative. From primary to secondary, all our curriculum plans require a clear thread of reading tuition.

Most reading for learning is non-fiction; our best higher reading teaching is through literature. It is this mismatch between need and offer that is at the heart of the difficulties of learning to read and reading to learn. The reading aspect of the curriculum starts well but needs development and broadening during a pupil's education.

Michael Marland is Headteacher of North Westminster Community School.

Fig. 8.2 Cutting from the *Guardian*, November 13 1990

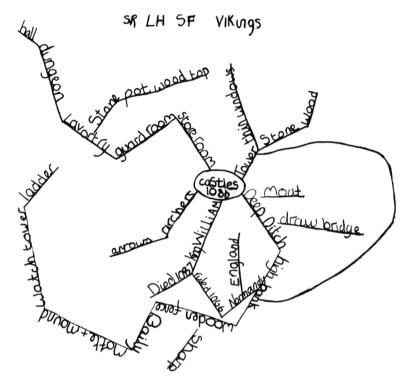

Fig. 8.3 'Brainstorming' to define the extent of knowledge and then used to devise quality questions

who? why? when? how? where? what? I then ask them to put these words together to make a question. With younger children I say the words for them:

'Why . . . whiskers . . . ? Think of a question?

Children might suggest:

'Why do cats have whiskers?'

'How do cats get whiskers?'

'Where do cats have whiskers?'

'What colour are cat's whiskers?'

The children are then asked to brainstorm to think of more questions. I ask them, in pairs, to generate as many questions as they can. At this stage I do not mind about the quality of questions: I want quantity. Giving children the structure of a question helps them greatly in this process. It is important that the children then put aside their questions for a few days, and only after this period do I ask them to assess the quality of their original questions. The children cross out any questions to which they already know the answers and those to which they think they could not easily find the answer. I find this 'weeding out' process helps their minds to really focus on these questions that are potentially good ones. They then go through the questions again and select the two questions which, as a pair, they would most like to pursue. The children now have a real purpose. They can search the books to see if they have the answer to their questions. They will be more likely to read actively.

TEACHING CHILDREN HOW TO USE INFORMATION BOOKS

Before children can make use of their questions they must become familiar with information books, and must know the differences between information books and narratives. They must know how to use information books and be able to judge which ones will be most helpful to them.

This is how I start to teach children the differences between informational and narrative text types. First I find out how much the children already know about information books and informational reading. I sit the children in a circle around me and I give each child an information book. I tell them that they have two minutes to find out everything they can about what is in the book. I tell them that they should be able to find sufficient information to talk about that subject for another three minutes. I then watch what the children do. How many of them start reading frantically from page one and try to get through as much as they can? Which children know how to survey their books?

Next, I ask the children to tell what their books are about: obviously those children who already know how to survey a text manage much better than those children who have tried to read from page one. Many teaching points concerning the layout of information books and the way to read them can come out of this activity.

I base my work with the children on an approach called 'SQ3R' originally developed for adults by Robinson (1962). SQ3R was developed to improved readers' ability to locate and use information in long passages of text and to improve comprehension. It involves readers directing their attention to text organisation. The S stands for Survey, the Q for Question and the Rs for Read, Review and Recite. I have found that for primary aged children the Surveying, Questioning and Reading are the most useful parts of the technique: the rest is too structured.

The Survey is a way of looking at a book in a thorough and detailed way. During a Survey children should be assessing whether the book will be of any use to them for their project work. Will they be able to find the relevant information easily? Will they be able to read the text? Is it likely to have the type of information that they want?

A Survey should include finding out the following information.

What is the title of the book?

What is the author's name?

Is there a useful blurb on the back? What does it say?

When was the book published?

What sort of illustrations does the books have?

Are there any captions? Read a few of them to see if they are helpful.

Is there a good table of contents? What does it tell you about the contents of the book?

Are there headings? Are they useful?

Is the introduction useful, if so how?

Is the index likely to help?

Is there a useful glossary?

The children check these features of the books that they are using or are likely to use. This gives them an initial impression of how useful each book might be. I then teach the children about structural guiders: which ones are really useful and in which circumstances? Can they judge whether one book is more useful than another for a particular task?

3

What we want to find out	Name of Book	Middle Ages	Living History	Castles Hired	Young History Book 2	Invaded Island	Story of...	Knights	People of Long Ago	Lewis Guide	Dana Code
NORMAN CASTLES:		✓	✓	X	X	X	✓	X	X	✓	X
VILLAGERS HOMES:		X	✓	X	X	X	✓	X	✓	X	X
FOOD IN NORMAN TIMES:		✓	X	✓	X	X	X	✓	X	X	X
PEOPLE LIVING IN CASTLES:		✓	✓	✓	X	X	X	✓	✓	X	X

Fig. 8.4   Children's matrix of books related to a particular project

The children then make a matrix of the books related to their project. Figure 8.4 on the previous page shows how the children record their intended areas of research down the left hand side of the matrix, and the books that might be helpful along the top. The books are given ticks or crosses according to whether they cover each sub-topic.

The children then make up a second matrix to record the number of structural guiders in each book. The children must be encouraged to question the use of structural guiders: does the presence of structural guiders make the book any more useful? An example of the second matrix is shown in figure 8.5 below.

	The Builder	William The Conqueror	Invaded Island	Looking At History? & The Middle Ages	Living History Bk?	Dover Castle Handbook	Lewes Castle Handbook	Castles (Jumbo)	Castles (Databank Series)	People Of Long Ago	Young Historian Book 2	Houses & Homes
BIBLIOGRAPHY:												
GLOSSARY:						✓			✓		✓	
INDEX:	✓		✓	✓					✓			
CONTENTS:	✓		✓	✓	✓	✓	✓	✓	✓		✓	
PICTURES:	✓	✓	✓	✓	✓	✓	✓	✓	✓	✓	✓	✓
PICTURE REFERENCES:				✓	✓	✓		✓	✓	✓		
COLOUR:	✓	✓	✓	✓				✓		✓	✓	✓
DIAGRAMS:	✓		✓	✓		✓	✓	✓	✓	✓	✓	✓
PHOTOGRAPHS:			✓	✓		✓	✓	✓	✓			
SKETCHES:			✓	✓	✓		✓	✓	✓	✓		
TITLE:	✓		✓	✓	✓	✓	✓	✓	✓		✓	✓
CHAPTERS:	✓		✓	✓	✓	✓	✓	✓	✓	✓	✓	
PAGE NUMBERS:	✓	✓	✓	✓	✓	✓	✓		✓		✓	✓
SUB-HEADINGS:			✓	✓	✓	✓	✓	✓	✓		✓	✓
READING:	✓	✓	✗	✓	?	✗	✓	?	✓	✓	?	✓
FINDING OUT:	✗	?	✗	✓	✓✓	?	✓	?	✓✓	✓	✗	✗

Fig. 8.5   Children's matrix listing the structural guiders in each book

The importance of headings in information books is worth pointing out to the children at this stage. As mentioned in Chapter 3, headings have a very important function in expository texts. Research with adults has shown that the mere presence of a heading in a text helps the reader's understanding (Dansereau, 1982; Dansereau, Brooks, Spurlin and Holley, 1979). Children need to realise that there are times when reading only the headings is an appropriate strategy.

The second part of the SQ3R process is Questioning. The art of good questioning and a possible approach to teaching it has already been covered earlier in the chapter.

The third part of the SQ3R process is Reading. The children must be taught to read a text in an active fashion to decide whether it is too hard for them or not. All too often Junior aged children think that they can read something if they can pronounce the words. I give such children an exercise similar to Activity 3 on page 29. This helps them to realise that some books are too hard for them. However, it does take older children some time to accept the idea that their reading ability alters according to the type of text that they have in front of them. Here again I find a matrix useful because the children can put a mark to indicate whether each text is hard or not.

I do not discourage children from using texts that are perhaps too hard, but I do suggest they become familiar with the concepts first by using other easier books. Very often books that were originally written for adults are easier to tackle than those written specifically for children.

PRIOR KNOWLEDGE

Chapter 1 emphasised the importance of prior knowledge in informational reading. It will be remembered that because young children often do not have the requisite prior knowledge it is important to bring to the fore the knowledge that they do have on the subject. The research on reading also suggests that if children can vocalise their thoughts about the text then their learning is likely to be more effective. For instance Judith Langer (1981) developed a useful prereading plan 'PReP' which involves heightening the prior knowledge of the reader by discussing what they know, and giving them help with concepts on which they are not so sure.

The work of McDonald (1978), Schwartz (1975) and Anderson, Spiro and Anderson (1978) with adults and older children also suggests that readers should be taught to ask questions about the text they are reading. I have found this to be so. If you ask children to predict what the text is about then their reading improves. Additionally, if you ask children to make up questions for other children, this helps them to become familiar with the ideas behind the text. It seems that these questioning activities force readers to encode the information more than they might if they simply reread it.

VARIOUS NOTEMAKING STRATEGIES

Mapping is another useful technique which encourages readers to bring their prior knowledge to the fronts of their minds before they read. This enables them to build bridges between their prior knowledge and the task ahead. First readers record all that they know on the subject (this is similar to the brainstorming activity discussed on pp. 130–33). Then they record what they expect to find in a particular chapter. The recording is done diagrammatically. When the text is finally read the new information is added to the diagram. This process is similar to mind mapping but in this instance the child adds information to the diagram from their reading.

It seems that it is the actual process of making the maps that is important. Just providing maps for the reader is not so successful (Meyer et al, 1980; Church, 1985; Armbruster and Anderson, 1982). I have tried this technique with older children however, and have found that once the children have learned how to model they no longer need to draw a diagram about what they already know, unless the text is very demanding. Modelling is a notemaking strategy discussed on pp. 158–79.

Mapping can, however, be a useful prelude to other forms of notemaking. Another technique is to put children into the situation of being researchers and reporters. For instance, if all the children in the class are finding out about castles and each group's task is to find out about a particular castle, then that group becomes the authority on that castle. Later each member of the group, except one, is sent off to one of the other groups with a note pad. These children act like reporters finding the information about the other castles. They make notes and bring the information back to their own group. The child left behind in each group has the task of reporting the group's findings to the visiting 'reporters'. This way not only do all the children get a real chance to research, but they see the point of asking their colleagues questions. They also tend to make meaningful notes. This approach is often called 'jigsawing'.

Before I discuss the various notemaking strategies I would like to reiterate three points.

First, it must not be forgotten that, on the whole, children are more unfamiliar with the expository text form. In the words of Morris and Stewart-Dore:

> Our schemata for narrative are far richer than those for expository material. Not only are we experienced in reading narrative forms, but these forms per se have functional structures (story grammars) which are far more familiar, more concrete and hence more predictable than expository text.
> (Morris and Stewart-Dore 1984) (Their use of the word 'schemata' in this context means conceptual understanding.)

Thus we have to wean our children off a diet of stories. Children must become familiar with informative books they must know how to change their reading to the task in hand and they must read with a pre-set question in mind.

Second, too many primary texts are so weakly designed that teaching children how to be effective readers can be a problem.

Children must be taught some form of notemaking, for it is important that they realise that they do not have to remember or record everything they read. The key to effective notemaking is being selective.

WHICH NOTEMAKING ACTIVITY IS MOST EFFECTIVE?

The answer to this question is not simple. Three points need to be borne in mind. First, some individuals find one strategy more helpful than another. Second, the effectiveness of a strategy depends on the task in hand. Third, readers must be given a variety of activities so that they can match strategy to purpose.

All the earlier American research on the subject of notemaking was reviewed by Anderson and Armbruster in 1982. They concluded that 'almost any technique *can* be effective', but the research also suggests that there is no one superior method. A number of notemaking techniques will now be discussed.

Summarising

This involves extracting key sentences or key thought units from a text. How this is to be done is never fully explained in the literature, but a good notemaker is one who can 'restate what the author said in a more concise form', with the main ideas and essential supporting details of a text being retained but the illustrative and elaborating statements left out.

Often, however, summarising is seen as a strategy whereby readers try to reconstruct the text by either copying words, sentences or even paragraphs down or trying to put them in their own words. In this section I am referring to the type of notes that are written in lines and usually follow the course of the original text. An example is given in figure 8.6 below.

Very little research on this type of notemaking has been carried out with primary school children. The one piece of in-depth research by Brown, Day and Jones (1983) in America concluded that young children are intellectually unable to make notes of this type. They found that by the age of 10 or 11 children could attempt written summaries but that the summaries were inadequate as working documents for the children to use. Any formal strategy that the researchers tried with this age group failed. The problem with this research was that the notemaking task was such a highly structured activity that it was little wonder that the children were unable to cope with it intellectually.

The research evidence on the effectiveness of summarising for adults is not much more encouraging. The reason for this could be that summarising does not demand deep level processing: readers are not put into a position where they have to understand the text fully. It is the process of going below the surface features of the text that enables the reader to learn (Anderson and Armbruster, 1982). Another disadvantage of summarising is that it does not involve the readers in reorganisation of the text. Summarising is also time consuming, and for young children it is tiring.

I have found over all that summarising is not very useful for children. It

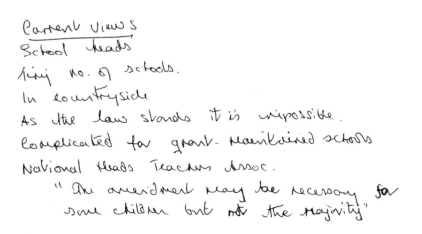

Fig. 8.6   Summarising in linear note form

does not help them to extract the essential information, and they very soon either give up or learn some variation of the technique that is closer to copying than to true information retrieval.

Outlining

Outlining is a development of summarising which requires readers to be able to follow a particular structure. Outlining is the recording of information from reading material in a way that makes clear the relationship between the main ideas and the supporting details. Although outlining has been taught in schools, I am not going to pursue it in any depth because the research suggests that it is very hard, and that it is no more successful than other strategies. It is certainly not suitable for young children.

Underlining

Underlining or some other form of text marking is a common practice amongst adults and students. In fact, with the advent of highlighter pens and photocopying facilities it is increasingly popular. We have all come across heavily marked library books!

Adults who use this technique have usually developed their own method of marking text: they were never taught. When challenged, the majority of adults realise that they have not really mastered all of the advantages of this technique, and most are willing to admit that their attempts are inefficient. Many adults have to re-read the whole of the text if they are to retrieve a particular item of information. Some adults admit to underlining far too much of the text to be helpful, while others never return to the underlined words. However, most adults like to underline because it aids concentration during reading.

The effectiveness of underlining is based on the 'Von Restorff Effect': the isolation of an item against a background that is homogeneous produces increased recall of that item. This observation is supported by the work of Fowler and Barker (1974). They found that if students marked their reading material they remembered it better than if they did not.

Little research has been carried out in this country into the benefits of underlining. None, to my knowledge, has been performed on primary children. However, research has been carried out in the States on older children and students. Anderson and Armbruster (1982) concluded that the research on underlining as a tool for adults and students is inconclusive. Some researchers suggest that it is effective while others suggest it is no more helpful than re-reading the text. This disparity of findings probably arose because the readers in each piece of research were given different instructions on how to mark the text. Adults usually mark too much of the text. It seems from the work of Stordahl and Christenstein (1956) and Idstein and Jenkins (1972) that when students were allowed to underline as much as they wished, the markings were of little or no help to them, but if they were limited as to the number of words they could underline they remembered significantly more.

Again it seems that it is the actual process of marking the text that is helpful to readers, because if they are given pre-lined texts the results are less encouraging (McAndrew, 1983).

Underlining was first used with secondary children by Lunzer, Gardner, Davies and Greene (1984). This work suggested that underlining could be of real benefit to older pupils. I have since adapted the idea and used it very successfully with primary children.

How I teach underlining

When I am teaching a class of children how to make notes I always start with underlinings, as it can be learnt very quickly and brings immediate gains in notemaking skills. It is of benefit in its own right but I have found that it is more effective when it is used in conjunction with other note-making skills (as explained later in the chapter).

Any age group of children can learn to underline effectively. It is a skill that encourages active reading and enables children to search for answers to pre-set questions. Most importantly it shows children how the text can become redundant. At this juncture I must reassure you that I am not going to encourage you to allow the children to deface the school's books! I suggest using acetate film, which is available in different qualities. I have found the middle- to high-quality is most suitable. The teacher can prolong the life of this acetate by attaching card on two edges. This can be fixed by glue or staple. These sheets are fastened to the relevant pages by paper clips, and fine-nibbed, non-permanent marker pens (available in various colours) are used for the underlining. By using a damp cloth, the underlining can be altered or wiped away.

Children must be taught how to be effective underliners. I tell the children how important it is to be able to extract just certain words – the ones that will enable them to remember what the text was about. I reiterate the importance of making some parts of the text redundant. I also teach the children always to ask a question when they are underlining. This questioning will make them active readers. If the book has headings then the children can turn these headings into questions by using the question words *who? what? why? when? how?* and *where?*

I give the children a maximum number of words that they are allowed to underline. The number of words underlined must be limited quite strictly at the beginning, for example I might insist on no more than 15 words on a particular page. Later the children learn to limit themselves.

I have found that by limiting children to a specific number of words they view the task as a precise job and are often too absorbed with counting and finding 'the correct words'. This obsession soon wears off and once the children start to rewrite their underlined words, they soon see the real reason for limiting the number of words.

I have experimented with the underlining technique and I found that very young children are able to carry out this task. It may sound strange to some of my readers but I have found that it is far more successful if the children are not asked to read the text aloud. I have found that having to pronounce the words actually gets in the way of reading to understand. If some children are a little unsure of the task they get help from their partner.

I have found that the success of this activity depends on getting the children to talk about the text, this is why they work in pairs. When children work on their own I find that the task is done in seconds, with little thought, but if told that they will have to come to a consensus on the best 10 words to underline, the children will work quite happily on the task for a lengthy period. The activity creates a lot of discussion and the children are using their language to interact with the text. Also they have much more confidence in themselves when they are working together and are more likely to argue later for their choice of underlined words. It is very important to allow the children to get together as a large group after they have worked in pairs, so that they can learn that there is no one set of ten words that is right. Some sets are better than others, but words that are meaningful or memorable to one pair are not necessarily so for another.

The most important outcome of underlining is that children begin to appreciate that large parts of a text can be made redundant. Having the confidence to abandon parts of the text is likely to help them to make effective notes. I have written about the importance of reading for a purpose elsewhere in the book and Activity 6 on p. 130 shows that we read for different purposes.

Once the children have underlined the words I ask them to list them on a scrap of paper. They then use this piece of paper as their notes. The words are left for a few days before the children are asked to write up from these notes.

It has been found in some of the schools that I have worked in that successful texts can be put on to boards and then covered with acetate, so that the texts are permanently available in the resources room.

Strengths of underlining

1   It is easy for any age group to learn the technique.

2   Underlining can be used on any text.

3   It helps children to read more actively.

4   It helps children to read for a purpose.

5   It encourages children to read to answer a particular question.

6   Children using the technique are often willing to work on a text for a long time.

7   When children work in pairs on underlining, useful discussions develop.

8   The underlined words pinpoint the important part of the text.

9   Underlining teaches children to make parts of the text redundant.

10   Another advantage of underlining is that it highlights the importance of reading for a purpose. Readers can be asked to underline in different colours, the words that are important. For example, you could ask a class to underline in blue the parts of the text that tell you why swallows like to travel and in red the parts of the text that tell you what swallows eat. When you have asked different children to read for different purposes the coloured lines can be compared by putting the different pieces of acetate on top of each other. Excellent discussions can develop out of this activity.

11   Children enjoy using acetates and different coloured felt pens.

Weaknesses of underlining

Despite its many benefits, I have found that underlining does have its limitations. It is most useful when it is used in conjunction with other activities.

1   Underlining does not, on its own, demand the reader to reorganise the material, so real understanding may not be achieved. The reader retains the author's original words and structure.

2 If children have not understood why active reading is important, they will either guess, or worse still underline the words in the text that they do not understand. (Adults do the same.) All too frequently the reader never returns to really understand the text.

3 Another problem that can arise is that, even if the children have been taught to limit the number of words, when they are left to their own devices, they may underline too many words.

Sample underlining activities

The Domesday Book consists of two volumes: Little Domesday covering Essex, Suffolk and Norfolk, and the Great Domesday covering the rest of the country as far north as Yorkshire. Only Little Domesday is dated and opinions have varied as to when Great Domesday was completed; some even suggesting that it was as late as the reign of Henry I (1100–35).

The current view is that the information for both volumes was probably assembled by summer 1086 and possibly by August, when a great assembly was held at Salisbury. Production of the book could then have started in the winter. It had probably reached its final stages by September 9, 1087, when William died in Rouen. There follows some documents which are major pieces of evidence used to date Domesday.

At the end of Little Domesday, a note gives a precise date for the survey. 'In the year 1086 from the incarnation of the Lord, the twentieth of the reign of William, this survey was made not only through these countries but through the whole of England.' *The Anglo-Saxon Chronicle* provides a framework for dating the Domesday Book through two pieces of evidence. Firstly, the account of Christmas at Gloucester, when the king ordered the Domesday survey. This was probably done in the chapter house of the Cathedral. It shows that the survey was ordered in 1085 and that the records were brought to the king afterwards. Secondly, *The Anglo-Saxon Chronicle* describes the great assembly at Salisbury and Williams's movements during the last months he spent in England. Some sort of draft or return from the survey was probably brought to the king during this time.

Further evidence that the information for the Domesday Book was collected during William's lifetime comes from the book itself. Domesday describes property held by Geoffery, chamberlain to Mathilda the king's daughter, which he held for the service he performed to her. This information must have been collected before the kings death because William II had neither a wife nor a daughter.

Underline in blue the words that tell you how the woods are different from now.
Underline in red the questions that the survey asked.
Underline in yellow the answers that the questioners received.
Underline in black an example of a wood that existed in Domesday time.
Underline in orange those bits of text that tell you something you did not know before.

The following activity can be given to a group of children who are working on the Stone Age. (I have not included the text.)

Underline in blue the parts of the text that tell you what Stone Age people ate. No more than 6 words.
Underline in green the parts of the text that tell you what they made their weapons from. No more than 7 words.
Underline in orange the parts of the text that tell you where the Stone Age people may have lived and what they may have lived in. No more than 8 words.
Underline in red the parts of the text that tell you what animals the Stone Age man may have hunted. No more than 6 words.
Underline in purple the parts of the text that showed you how different life was in the Stone Age. No more than 10 words.

Figure 8.7 overleaf shows the pattern that one child produced as a result of this type of activity. Each branch line is a different colour. Figure 8.8 shows the child's written work on the same topic.

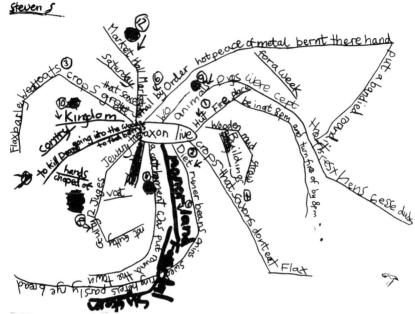

Fig. 8.7   Underlining as a way of selecting information

Crossing Out

This is a useful technique that I have developed for younger children, aged between 5 and 7 years, or for older children who have difficulties with reading to learn. It leads them neatly into underlining.

I take a piece of text from one of the childrens' primary information books – one that is relevant to their current project. I then add, every so often, some form of nonsense. I ask the children, in pairs, to cross out all those words that have nothing to do with the topic, without reading the text out loud. The funnier I can make the text, the better it works. I have found this activity to be very popular with children.

The children learn a great deal about redundancy of language through this activity. They also have to read the text for meaning. A slight disadvantage of the activity is that teachers do have to create the text for themselves, but it does not take long and the texts can then be used by successive groups of children. I include two examples of text (on p. 148) that I have used with 5 and 6 year-olds. Remember I do not ask the children to read out loud.

It concerns me to find that some quite 'capable' older readers often find

SAXONS. LIFE.

Saxon is a norman Slave, Saxons lived in huts made out of wood and mud they had a fire place inside, the fire hand to be of by 8pm and all the Saxons had to be in by 8pm. A Saxons diet is runner beans, oinions, swed, Sting netals, parsly, rye and bread, in the telids there grew Oats, weaht, and barly and flax, flax sias a metarel used to make baskets.

The Manor is a peace of land under the feudal system it has a church a farm and huts, when somone has done a murder to see if they are guilty or not guilty it is called trail by order the Juges would get a hot peace of metal and put it on the persons hand it would burn the hand and tee their would be a scar then the Juges would put a bandage

Fig. 8.8 Written work produced after selecting information by underlining

this task quite difficult – they cross out just one word or a pair of words but not the whole nonsense sentence. This is further evidence that so called 'good readers' often do not read for meaning.

Two examples of nonsense text used with 5- and 6-year-olds are given below, followed by one used with older children.

This text is about the Three Bears. Cross out those bits of text that have nothing to do with them.

Father Christmas is coming to home. Once upon a time there were three bears. XXXXXCCCC. They lived in a house deep in a wood. Ice cream chocolate and bananas. There was a father bear a mother bear and a baby bear. My name is Bob. BBBBBBB. One day they went out for a walk. When the bears were out a little girl came along her name was Goldilocks. I like cereal for breakfast. She went in their house and found three bowls of porridge. She tried father bear's porridge it was too lumpy. She tried mother bear's porridge it was too runny. She tried baby bear's porridge it was just right so she ate it all up. Yum Yum Yum Yum Yum Yum Yum Yum Yum Yum Yum Yum.

This text is about ears and how we hear, cross out everything else.

You have two ears. Your ears help you to hear sounds. Prince William has two arms and two legs. Animals have two ears. There was an old woman who lived in a shoe. It did not look like an ear. Inside your ear you have a drum which helps you hear the sounds.

> Find out about how Stone Age people lived.
> Cross out the irrelevancies and nonsense.
>
> Stone Age people found out how to make a fire. They did not like central heating. They twisted or rubbed a stick in a groove of another piece of wood, whilst watching television. The wood grew so hot that it set fire to pieces of dry grass and small twigs which came from the trees by a football pitch. A fire kept the family warm if the electric heater broke. It also frightened wild animals away.

A teacher explained to me how she had expanded upon the technique by using an April Fool's Day text from a newspaper. The children had believed all they had read about a monkey being born in an egg on their first reading. However, when the date was pointed out to the children and they realised they had been tricked, they then had great fun crossing out those parts of the text that had been made up.

Tabulation

In American literature this technique is known as MOAN which stands for Matrix, Outlining and aNalysis. It is a technique which requires the children to read for meaning in order to create a chart. The children either decide on the most appropriate headings themselves or use a prepared chart, and then put the information into the correct boxes in note form. The children will not be able to create the chart for themselves until they have had practice with teacher-created tables. If the technique is used correctly the original information will be totally reorganised. Thus the children will be able not only to learn from the chart, but also to make comparisons that were not apparent in the original text.

Some topics are more suitable for tabulation than others: the best ones are those that involve some sort of comparison or classification. Most texts on nature are suitable, as are those on buildings such as houses and flats, or those texts that compare people or groups of people.

I have found that this technique is most effective if the children work in pairs until they are really familiar with its demands. The valuable discussions generated by the activity are one of its major benefits, so it is important that it is not carried out in isolation. I have found that the individuals within the pairs can be of quite differing reading abilities but the activity will still work well.

If the children are used to underlining, they can underline the text first and then transfer their underlined words to the matrix. Unless the children have had plenty of notemaking practice they will need to be told that there is a limit to the number of words they can put in each cell, or they often copy verbatim and lose the real value of the exercise. Sometimes it is appropriate to ask the children to put a model in each of the cells instead of words (see Modelling).

It is important to prepare material for this activity as realistically as possible. If children are given texts on separate pieces of paper with, for instance, the text on each tree being on a different page and the matrix on a separate page, the task becomes realistic. They see it as being like 'office work', and they enjoy moving from one piece of text to another.

Once the matrix has been completed it can be used in all sorts of ways. For instance with the cat tabulation in figure 8.9 opposite, I ask the children how many cats are from a certain country, or how many cats are loving. I find that young children really enjoy this type of reorganisation.

I have been surprised and delighted by the writing that children have created from a table. I usually ask them to complete the table on one day then put aside the work for two or three days, the original text being taken away. The children are then required to use their charts as a starting point for their write-up. They find it really helpful because all the organisation has already been done. It is surprising how easy the children find the writing up task: all they need do is put in more elaborating language. I have found that the writing is usually in the right register – the register of an information text. There are no unnecessary words.

This shows that, armed with appropriate strategies, children can totally reorganise a text and produce something with a different structure. The finished product is a form of summary but it shows understanding. However, I do not think children should be asked to use their table as a tool for writing up every time. The activity of making a table is often sufficiently demanding in itself; the children learn by creating it and certainly improve their reading.

The mushroom example in figures 8.10a and b overleaf, shows how a seemingly difficult text can become accessible to children if they are given the right tasks.

Figures 8.11a and b on p. 153, show pieces of writing from two children in Year 3 whose first language is not English. Fig 8.12 on p. 154, shows a Year 3 child's writing about a Horse Chestnut tree.

what type of cat	where the cat came from	colour of cat	loving or not loving	what is special about the cat

Long-haired White

These cats came from a large place called Asia. They make very clean and gentle pets. Some of these cats have blue eyes if they do they will be deaf.

Long-haired White

Burmese

These cats came from a country called Burma. They are a brown colour. They used to be called Sacred Temple cats. These cats were very important and if a slave let the cat die the slave would also die. They are clever cats and are very loving.

British Blue

This is a cat that has short hair. It comes from Britain. It is intelligent and loving. The good thing about this cat is that it will not scratch your furniture. They will become good friends with dogs. They will like going for walks.

British Blue

Fig. 8.9   Reorganising material by tabulation

Mushrooms.

8. *Clitocybe inversa*

This too is a 'funnel-shaped fungus', but the shape is more obvious. The cap, up to 10 cm wide, is clearly hollowed out in the middle.

The colour of the cap is between reddish brown and a light yellow-brown, with light brown gills extending well down the yellowish stem. This species can be found in autumn, usually in colourful groups, in all kinds of woods. They often remain whole far into the winter.

The specimens illustrated are light coloured because of a drought.

15–16. *Boletus erythropus*

This boletus looks very similar to a highly poisonous variety. (15) shows a young example, and (16) is older. The layer of tubes and part of the stem or stipe are a fiery red. The thick, fleshy cap is hemi-spherical to dome-shaped with a yellowish brown skin. The stem is robust and varies in colour from yellow to orange to red, with red patches and red wrinkles. The spores are yellowish brown. It can be found from June to October in all kinds of woods and along country paths.

5. The sickener *Russula emetica*

The cap is round at first, flattened later, and is up to 12 cm across. It is purplish or pink; the gills are white and the stem

white with some pink. This toadstool is not deadly poisonous, but it causes horrible sickness.

19. *Cordyceps ophioglossoides*

Club-shaped fruit bodies like this are rare. If the fruit body is reddish black, covered with fine spikes on the upper side, then it is a parasite on another fungus, the underground truffle, *Elaphomyces muricatus*. Other species live as parasites on insect larvae (page 13).

The *Elaphomyces muricatus* grows underground, has a potato-like sporophore, and is not found wild in this country.

17. *Boletus scaber*

The mycelium of this useful boletus enables birches to obtain water and additional minerals from the soil. It also breaks down organic remains, even in dry sandy soil. The cap is a shallow dome with a yellow or dark brown skin. The layer of fine tubes is fairly shallow and usually covered with fine white scales. The edible white flesh becomes grey when exposed to air. The spores are light brown.

18. *Coltrichia perennis*

This is one of the few members of the bracket fungi which does not grow only on wood. The hairy cap is funnel-shaped, the skin brown, with concentric dark rings and a lighter coloured margin. Under the cap is a layer of spore tubes. The short stem is brown, with a thickened foot. The entire toadstool is leathery. It grows in groups from July to November, either on the ground or on pinewood, but usually in sandy soil.

Most other bracket fungi grow on dead or living wood.

7. Cheese cap
Clitocybe nebularis

This belongs to a group of 'funnel-shaped' fungi, though the toadstool cap is not clearly funnel-shaped. The cap is hemi-spherical at first, then flattened with a bump in the middle, and only later becomes funnel-shaped.

The skin of the cap is ash grey to white. When young it looks as though it has been dusted with flour. The stem is solid at first and hollow later. The flesh is white and has a sour unpleasant taste. This toadstool can be found in woods between September and November, often in fairy rings among fallen oak leaves.

Name	Place found	colour of the cap	height grows to	what is strange	poisonous/ taste	Latin names

Fig. 8.10a and b   Reorganising material by tabulation can make difficult text accessible to children

DUCK

A duck is a bird.
A Female duck is brown.
A male duck is green arnd wite and blue.
All the ducks drink water and all the ducks
eat bread. Duck have got Feathes on their
body. And they got little ears. Ducks have
got webbed Feet to help them swim.
Ducks have got a long beak. Ducks live
in the water.
Ducks kept on a farm are kept in the
stable at night to stop Foxes eating them.

Fig. 8.11a   Writing from a chart by a bilingual nine year old

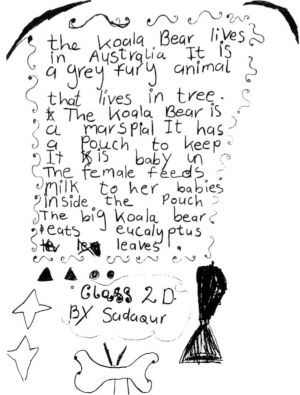

the koala Bear lives
in Australia It is
a grey fury animal
that lives in tree.
The koala Bear is
a marspial It has
a Pouch to keep
It is baby un
The female feeds
milk to her babies
inside the Pouch
The big koala bear
eats eucalyptus
leaves

Class 2 D.
BY Sadaqur

Fig. 8.11b   Writing from a chart by a bilingual eight year old

Horsechestnut Tree

The Horsechestnut tree grows in the United States, Great Britain and Europe. The fruit of a horsechestnut tree is a conker and children use them to play with. The flowers bloom in spring time. When it comes near the end of May the flowers begin to die. The colour of the flowers that grow on the tree are white with red spots. The type of wood that comes from a horsechestnut tree is soft and straight grained wood and the tree likes to grow in parks, woods, gardens, town squares, churchyards and village greens. The horsechestnut tree can grow up to about 20m in height. The seeds are spread by the conkers that grow on the tree in the Autumn and then fall off.

by

Nichola Harris

30. Horse chestnut *Aesculus hippocastanum*

The horse chestnut is not related to the sweet chestnut. It is a large tree, reaching 20 m in height, with an arched crown and drooping twigs (30a). On the twigs scars of fallen leaves can be seen, as well as the sticky plump buds (30b). The leaves unfold at the beginning of May, and at first they are hairy. Flowering also is in May, and the tree is full of 'candles' (30c and 30d). Not all the seeds in the big, three-celled fruits develop properly. The fruit-wall is covered with prickles; when it falls from the tree it splits and releases the chestnut brown seeds ('conkers'). They have a grey mark in the middle, where they were attached to the inside of the fruit (30f), and this is called the 'navel'.

The wood is not valuable, but the tree has been planted along many roads and in parks because it is so attractive. The tree casts a lot of shade, and is not suitable for small gardens.

Fig. 8.12   The original text with a Year 3 child's rewritten version

Fig 8.13 overleaf, shows a Year 5 child's work on the Thames Barrier: (a) shows part of the original text, (b) shows the table and (c) shows the final copy which was produced after a first draft.

Strengths of tabulation

1   Tabulation is a really useful strategy for children because the heading at the top of each category helps them to question the text.

2   When tabulating, children read actively and have a real purpose.

3   Tabulation raises the children's reading ability because it involves very specific reading tasks.

4   Children will quite happily read and re-read the same text when tabulating. Each time they are reading with a different purpose. They keep interacting with the information but the text does not become dull.

5   When using the technique, children are constantly skimming to get the gist of the text and scanning to re-find their place in the text. As a result, flexible reading habits are fostered.

6   The technique helps children to appreciate that text can become redundant: only the bare minimum goes into each cell.

7   The technique is very popular with children.

8   Using this strategy, the children learn to classify information. This helps their intellectual development.

9   Often some cells in the matrix cannot be filled in from the information given in the texts. This is an important concrete lesson for children: they can put a cross in the cell which signifies 'data not in text'. Children are often too hesitant to fault the text and this technique gives them confidence.

10 Tabulation can be used as a quick diagnostic tool: the teacher can quickly judge which children have not fully understood the text.

Weaknesses of Tabulation

1   Tabulation can only be used on certain kinds of text: unless the text contains information that can be classified, the other notemaking techniques will be more useful.

The Barrier

The Thames Barrier is the world's largest movable flood barrier. It has taken 4,000 men and women all over Britain eight years to build at a cost of nearly £500 million.

It was one of the largest, most difficult and most successful civil engineering projects in British history. It was conceived, designed and built by British engineers and – with only a few exceptions – the materials and parts have been produced and supplied by British industry. The Barrier was constructed and fitted by a largely British workforce and in terms of new technology and its application the Barrier has broken new ground. It is already being described as the eighth wonder of the world and its stainless steel roofs rival Tower Bridge as a pictorial symbol of London.

The Barrier spans a third of a mile across the Thames. It consists of 10 separate movable steel gates placed end to end across the river. The gates are pivoted and supported between nine concrete piers and two abutments which house the hydraulic machinery powering the gates.

The foundations of each of the main central piers are about as big as the main foundation for a power station. The piers and sills together contain half a million tonnes of concrete, enough to build a nine mile length of six-lane motorway.

When raised the four main gates each stand as high as a five storey building, as wide as the opening of Tower Bridge and weigh over 3,700 tonnes – more than a Type 42 destroyer. They are powered by the Barrier's own generators on the south bank which produce enough electricity to supply a small town.

Once the flood threat passes the gates swing down and lie horizontally in the river bed – recessed in pre-cast concrete sills, the largest of which are half the size of a football pitch. This allows shipping to navigate the Thames normally through the openings between the piers.

6

Fig. 8.13a   The original text

Nightingale Primary School

Building the Barrier

Number of people	Cost	Number of years	Number of gates	Height and weight and width of gates	Number of drawings/plans
4,000 men and women +	$500 million +	8 years. + date: 1974	10 gates	weight = 3,700 tonnes / Height = as high as a 5 storey building / width = of gates = opening Tower bridge. X	7000 +
			✓		
			✓		

Fig. 8.13b   The child's chart

Building the Barrier.

To build the barrier it took 8 years. they needed 4,000 people. Ten of them were women. Now thay have only 65 people working there. To build the barrier they needed £500 million. They started building in 1972. They had to build Ten gates for it. Each gate was built as high as a 5 storey building. The weight of each was was 3,700 tones. It was built as wide as the opening tover of bridge.

Fig. 8.13c   The child's written work

2   Children tend to copy chunks of text word-for-word into the cells unless they are taught that only three or four words are acceptable in each cell.

3   At first the teacher has to provide a blank table and either multiple copies of a book or photocopies of the relevant pages. The teacher must also spend time searching through books to find suitable pieces of text.

4   Children need practice before they can produce their own columns. They tend to produce columns that give little information at first: they must be allowed to make these mistakes.

Comparison across books

This technique which is the application of tabulation to several texts helps children to understand that what they read may not be accurate, and to develop a healthy scepticism for anything in print.

I provide a chart for the children on a subject such as, say, blackbirds. I ask the children to fill in the cells of the chart using four or five books. They often find that the books are not in agreement on certain points. The blackbirds topic is a good example: the books that I have used with children are inconsistent about the number of eggs laid, the material from which blackbirds build their nests, the times at which they build them and their preferred nesting places. As Shirley Paice (1984) found when she looked at books on honeybees, there is a surprising amount of inaccuracy in children's books.

Figure 8.14 opposite, shows part of a chart made by children to show the variety of foods in the Norman diet. All of the eight books used gave different information on what was on offer to the Normans.

Modelling

There are several variations on this technique, such as networking, schematising, idea mapping, and conceptual mapping. They are all, like modelling, strategies for representing the text in some graphical way. As noted earlier, altering the author's words and reorganising the information were the two main problems identified by adult notemakers. Modelling overcomes both of these problems.

I have found modelling to be one of the most effective reading and writing tools for children. They can immediately see the relevance of the technique and they quickly learn to use it. Modelling really helps children to gain meaning from a text.

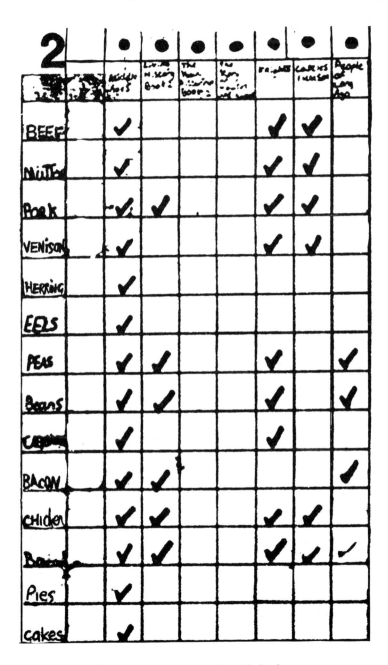

Fig. 8.14   The Norman diet as described in eight books

The technique involves reading a piece of text and then (instead of making traditional notes with words), representing the information in another way.

Teaching modelling

I give the children a piece of text from a relevant book, with any original illustrations taken away. They are then asked to make 'notes' on the piece of text without using any words: they might produce a picture or sketch (the easiest form for young children). Older children might represent the information as a line graph, a block graph, a time line, a flow diagram, a map, a scatter graph, a pie graph, a venn diagram, a cycle, a chart or any other concoction they can think of: I make no strict rules as long as the children are reading for meaning. When the children have become accustomed to the activity I do allow them to add a certain number of words, as this helps them to represent more abstract concepts.

I find that the children benefit from seeing each other's models, so at the end of a session I ask them to show me their models and we lay them out on a table so that we can compare the different representations. I try not to make judgements at this stage, it discourages more divergent thinking. I always do a model myself and show it to the children, but very often at least one child has thought of a better way to represent the material than myself.

When I introduce modelling into the classroom I give the children very little guidance on the activity, as I want them to be as creative as possible. I might ask them to represent the information in the text in such a way that a person who cannot read at all would be able to understand it. I tell the children that they must in some way change the words of the text to another form. I do find that some children need help with adding labels and making simple sequences. I always choose a piece of text that is relevant to their current project, so that they can bring their prior knowledge to the fore.

One interesting observation from my work on modelling is that young children take to the technique much more quickly than older ones. I have found that children aged between 5 and 7 accept the principles without question and immediately see the value of the activity, while older children take time to change their reading habits. All too often I find that the older children are only reading superficially.

A disadvantage of modelling is that not all texts lend themselves to it, so the text must be carefully chosen. When choosing a text teachers should try to produce their own representation first, since only by doing this will they see the problems that might face the children. The texts that suit modelling are those that describe an object, or a process, activity or character.

Unlike underlining and tabulation, modelling seems to work best if the children work on their own. It is also important that the teacher does not interact with the child until the model is complete, because the finished model is a window on the child's process of comprehension. By looking at it carefully, one can almost get into the mind of the child.

Activity 7

To understand the modelling process fully you should try it yourself, so quickly try to make notes on the following text without using any words.

> You should brush and comb your dog each day. Give your pet a blanket in its basket. Dogs need plenty of exercise. Take your dog for a walk each day. It will need a collar and lead. A puppy needs four meals a day. An older puppy needs only two meals a day. Feed your dog with meat and biscuits, and give it a fresh bowl of clean water to drink.
>
> Dogs can be given large bones to gnaw. Dogs should not be given small bones which splinter as these little splinters might get caught in their throat.

I suspect that you had problems representing some of these words. I have asked numerous teachers to model this piece of text and nobody has yet come up with an idea as good as Philip's for representing the words 'each day' (see figure 8.15 overleaf). He was only six and this was his first attempt at modelling.

Philip came up with the idea of representing 'each day' with seven leads and seven brushes. When he had finished the model I asked him about the little bones and he said 'Oh yes, it's there stuck in the dog's throat'. Modelling is a great technique for teaching children how to make notes, but another of its strengths is that it shows the teacher whether the child has really understood or not.

My second example of a model is one in which the child has mis-interpreted the text (see figure 8.16 on p. 163). Peter was obviously reading the text line by line and not seeing it as a whole. He had been working on birds with his class and he had been asked to read through the whole of the following passage before doing any drawing. However, all reasonable thoughts seem to have eluded this eight year old as he has the chick hatching and retreating three times!

> Inside the egg the chick begins to grow. It eats the yolk and grows bigger and bigger, until it fills the shell. It is then ready to hatch out. The chick has a tiny tooth on the end of its beak called an egg tooth.

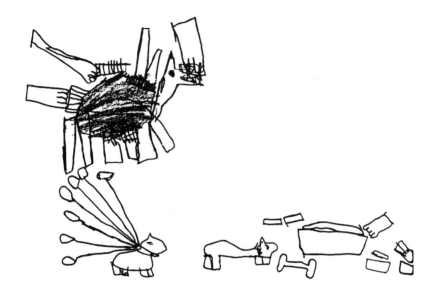

Fig. 8.15   Philip's model of how to look after a pet dog

> The tiny bird taps at the shell with its egg tooth when it is ready to
> hatch. The shell begins to crack and the chick starts to push with its
> head. The shell breaks apart and the chick rests before it struggles
> free. The tooth drops off. The chick is wet at first but soon dries off
> and becomes soft and fluffy.
> (The Life of Birds by M. Burton)

Peter's teacher had thought he was a very fluent reader, and found it hard to
believe that he was not understanding the text. However, when given a
different text Peter made similar mistakes: he seemed to be reading
sentence-by-sentence and not seeing the text as a whole. The quotation
from Grellet (p. 41) stated that if reading is to be efficient, longer units or
the whole text must be understood by the reader: this is obviously not the
case for Peter.

Figure 8.17 overleaf, shows the work of Joanne, who did understand the
text although she has used too many words. It was work like hers that suggested to me that children should complete their first models with no words
at all – otherwise they are still tempted to copy.

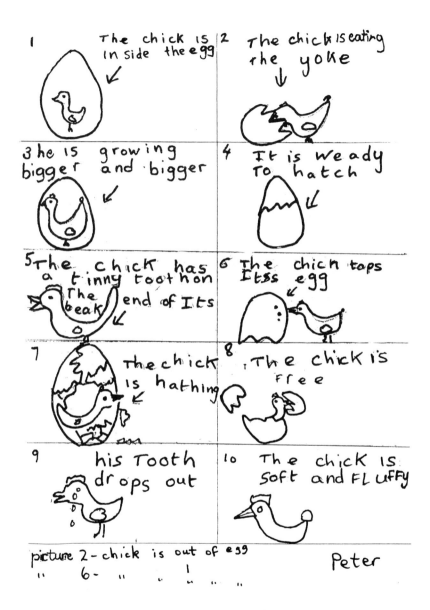

1 The chick is inside the egg

2 The chick is eating the yoke

3 he is growing bigger and bigger

4 It is weady To hatch

5 The chick has a tinny tooth on The beak end of Its

6 The chicn taps Itss egg

7 The chick is hathing

8 The chick is free

9 his Tooth drops out

10 The chick is soft and FLuffy

picture 2 - chick is out of egg
" 6 - " " " " "

Peter

Peter

Fig. 8.16   Peter's model of how a chick hatches

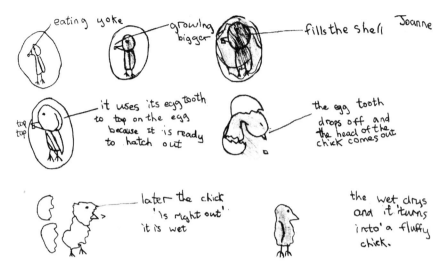

Fig. 8.17   Joanne's model of how a chick hatches

A major advantage of modelling is that it helps the teacher understand the processing level of bilingual children. Figure 8.18 opposite shows how two ten-year-olds misunderstood the word 'courtyard' in the following passage and became confused. The teacher did not realise until this point that the children were not speaking English at home.

> The Goblin and Mr Uppity passed through the gates and into a courtyard and through some more gates and along a long corridor and through some large gold doors and into a large room.

Modelling also shows up the defects in a text. The text below was given to a class of children aged seven and eight. They had been doing a project on planting, but many of them were thrown by the poor language of the text and drew at their first attempt a hole in the bottom of the pot – not as is logical, but as the text actually states (see figure 8.19 overleaf).

> Fill two plant pots with soil.
> Make a hole in each with a pencil.
> Put a brown apple pip in one hole
> and an orange pip in the other.
> Cover them with soil. Keep the soil damp.
> Place them on a sunny window sill.
> Soon you will see some green shoots growing.
> They will grow into a small apple tree and a small orange tree.

Fig. 8.18 This model shows how easily ten-year-olds can misunderstand a seemingly simple text

This text is a good example of a simplified text, probably written with readability formulae in mind. Simplified text like this can actually make the concepts more difficult to understand.

I could give many more examples of children's misunderstanding of various texts. In fact, children's mistakes on modelling tell us more about the reading process than their successes: it is often the familiar words that throw them. This leads me back to the work of Katharine Perera, who found that one of the difficulties children have with information texts is their use of words that have both a familiar and a specialised meaning. The following text illustrates the problem.

> Most beetles are vegetarians, and there is a beetle to eat almost every sort of plant. There is a huge family of leaf beetles, each with its favourite food. Popular beetles and willow beetles eat large holes in popular and willow leaves . . .

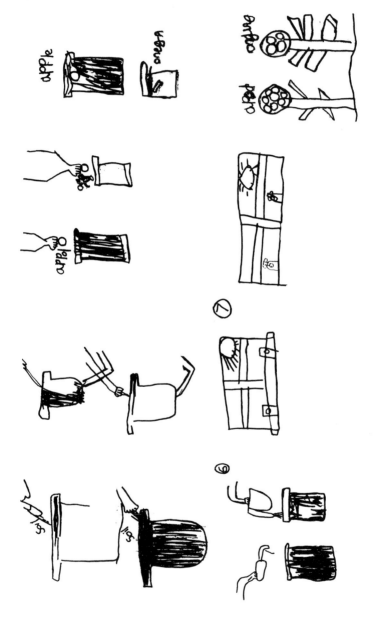

Fig. 8.19   Model showing how a child misinterpreted a poorly written text

Often the children's model from this piece of text consists of a drawing of Mummy beetle, Daddy beetle, and the baby beetles. The words that the children find difficult are not the words that we as adults expect. However, the most worrying aspect of mistakes like this is that children make them even though the text is on their current project.

I would also like to include another model (see figure 8.20 overleaf) from a six year old who has made a good attempt at a representation of the following text.

> Think About Hot and Cold.
> Our earth is warmed by the sun.
> In summer, the sun is nearest to us. Its rays bring warmth.
> In winter, the sun is farther away. Its rays bring less warmth.
> Air from a hairdryer is hot. Bathwater is warm.
> Snow is cold and so is ice.
> On a cold day, hot drinks help to make us feel warm.
> On a hot day, cold drinks help to keep us cool.
> Near the South Pole, the land is always covered with ice and snow.
> It is so cold, that few animals or birds can live there.
> A desert is so hot, that few animals or birds can live in it.

Modelling is in my view a very valuable learning tool. To create models, children must go below the surface of the text and keep re-reading the text using flexible reading strategies. Children really remember their models because they all look so different. However it is most important that the children are encouraged from the outset not to overvalue the representations themselves. They should be seen as working documents or notes.

I have been surprised to find how useful a model is as a method of notemaking, but if the children want to use it in this way it is best to make it into a two part process as with tabulation. On one day the children draw the model from the text. The original text is then taken away and the child's model is put aside for a few days. The children then write up notes from their model.

Here are some examples. The first one is by two Year 3 children. Figure 8.21a, b and c (pp. 169–171) show the original text underlined, the model and the first draft. The second model shown in figure 8.22 (on p. 172), is by a 5 year-old. The third model shown in figure 8.23 (on p. 173) is by two children who speak Sylheti at home but who operate in English at school. They have read the text in English, drawn a model, and then elaborated the picture using their own language.

The fourth example shows four children's work from the same original text. Figure 8.24a, b, c and d, shows how different each child's work is. The

Fig. 8.20   A six-year-old child's attempt at modelling

Whenever strangers approached, a long, brightly coloured curtain was hung up right across the tent from back to front, suspended in the centre from one of the main poles, making two "rooms". In a two-pole tent, these would be of unequal sizes; the male guests were entertained by the host and his sons in the larger side.

Women's side
The men did not intrude into the other side. The younger women and girls stayed out of sight behind the curtain, listening avidly to what was said, and peeping over whenever they thought they wouldn't be noticed. This side contained all the utensils for food preparation and cooking: the grindstones, cauldrons and wooden bowls. Women rarely sat idle; when they were not busy with other tasks they spun wool on their spindles. There were straw mats on the earth, often with sheepskins for sitting on, and a row of storage sacks for grain or dates, covered by a coloured woven carpet. A wooden chest held the best clothes and other treasures. The men's part was made beautiful with coloured carpets on the straw mats. The men rested their backs against the storage sacks which were covered with the best carpets. Camel saddles would be on this side, and if the host owned a horse, its saddle would have pride of place.

Fireplaces
In Arabian tents, there was a hollowed-out fireplace in the centre of the men's part, round which they sat on winter's nights and where coffee was made. In the Sahara, a small container of glowing embers would be brought in and placed on a bare patch of earth when tea was about to be brewed.

Fig. 8.21a   The original text on the Bedouin's underlined by the child

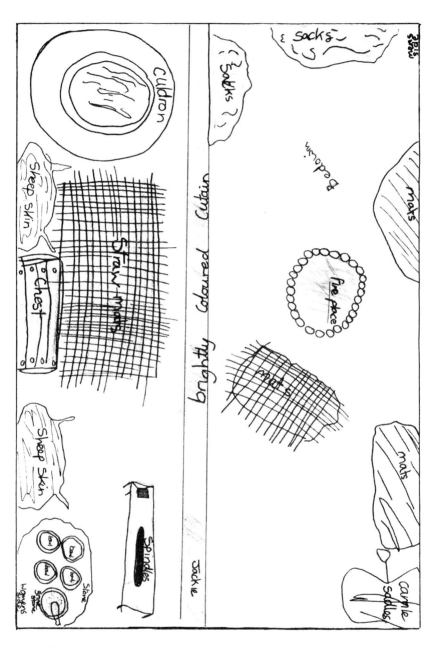

Fig. 8.21b   The model of a Bedouin tent

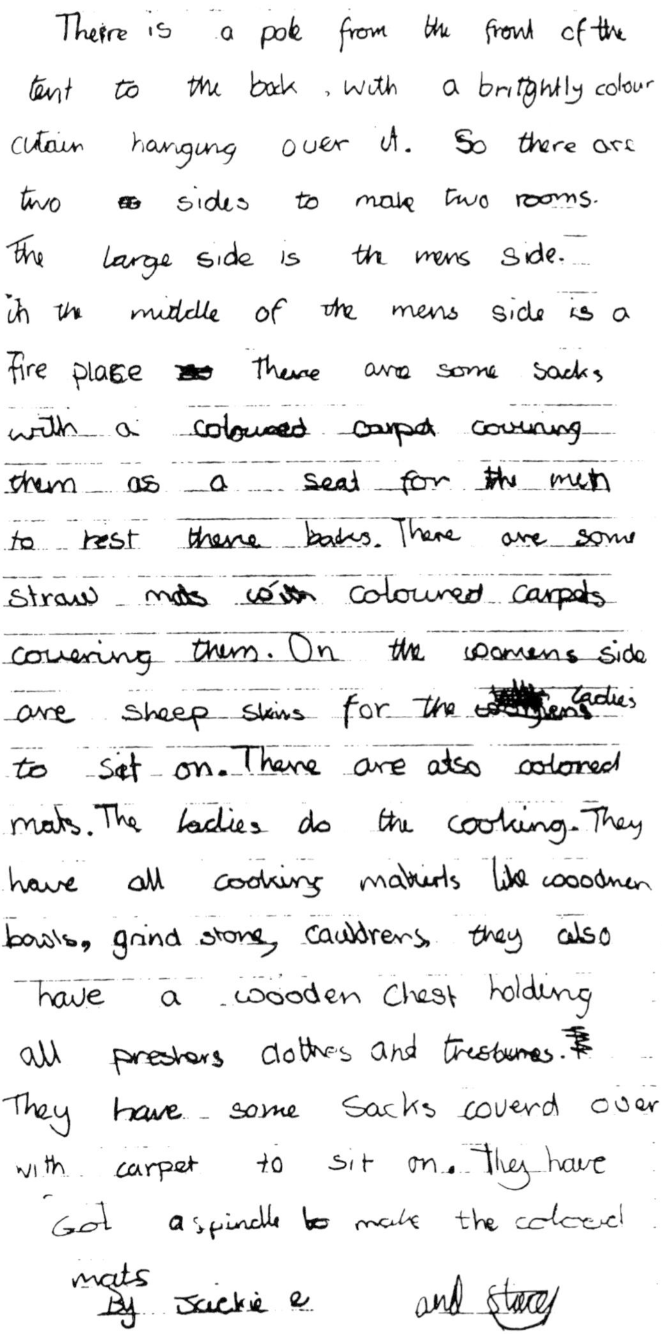

There is a pole from the front of the
tent to the back, with a brightly colour
curtain hanging over it. So there are
two sides to make two rooms.
The large side is the mens side.
In the middle of the mens side is a
fire place There are some sacks
with a coloured carpet covering
them as a seat for the men
to rest there backs. There are some
straw mats with coloured carpets
covering them. On the womens side
are sheep skins for the ladies
to set on. There are also coloured
mats. The ladies do the cooking. They
have all cooking materials like wooden
bowls, grind stone, cauldrens, they also
have a wooden chest holding
all prestors clothes and treasures.
They have some sacks coverd over
with carpet to sit on. They have
got a spindle to make the coloured
mats
By Jackie e and Stacey

Fig. 8.21c   Work produced one week after the underlining activity

Water

Water is used for all sorts of things.

We use water for washing ,we use it in the bath ,

we use it in the basin for our hands and faces, we

use it for washing up the dishes.

Fig. 8.22a and b   Original text and a model produced by a five-year-old

most pleasing aspect of this work is that the classteacher does not receive 30 pieces of writing all with the same structure.

Children find it quite easy to write up from their models. The models seem to provide a scaffold on which the children can structure their writing, and of course they can use their own words without the original author's words interfering.

It is interesting that so-called poor readers very often learn modelling and some of the other notemaking techniques far better than their fluent colleagues. It seems that they take more care with their reading, and even though they are slow they really try to make sense of the text. Many of the older juniors that I have worked with have got into bad habits and actually

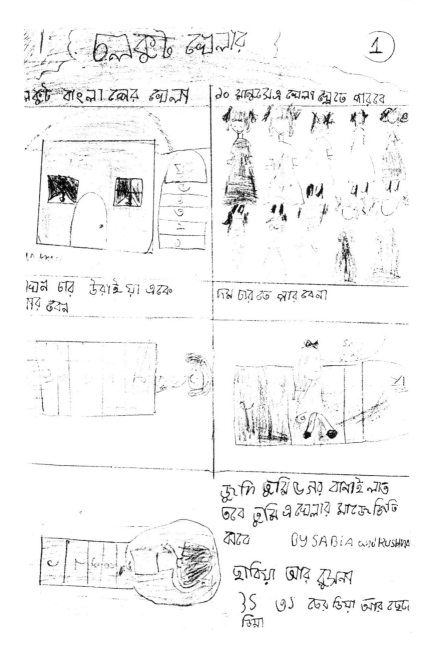

Fig. 8.23   A model with an accompanying Sylheti script

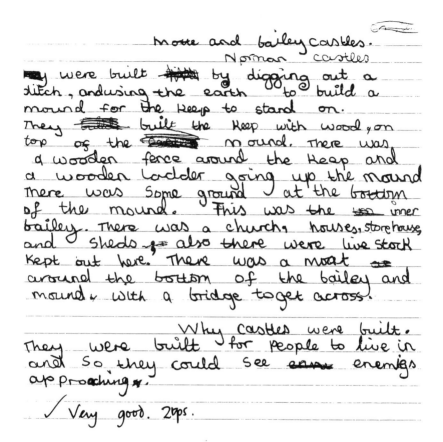

Motte and bailey castles.

Norman castles

They were built ~~____~~ by digging out a ditch, and using the earth to build a mound for the keep to stand on. They ~~____~~ built the keep with wood, on top of the ~~____~~ mound. There was a wooden fence around the keep and a wooden ladder going up the mound. There was some ground at the bottom of the mound. This was the ~~___~~ inner bailey. There was a church, houses, storehouse, and sheds ~~__~~ also there were live stock kept out here. There was a moat ~~__~~ around the bottom of the bailey and mound, with a bridge to get across.

Why castles were built.

They were built for people to live in and so they could see ~~____~~ enemies approaching.

✓ Very good. 2½ps.

Fig. 8.24a Modelling was used as a form of notemaking. Note how each child's work in Fig. 8.24 a, b, c and d is structured differently.

find reading for meaning very hard. As a general rule, older children are more likely to see the task as a drawing activity rather than a reading one, and take longer to adapt. Younger children do not have any preconceptions about reading, and so they adapt more quickly. This is supported by the work of Geva (1983).

It is important to stress to children at the very beginning that they do not have to be good at drawing in order to model. In fact as soon as a teacher starts valuing a model as a product rather than as part of the learning process, children start to be conscious of their drawing rather than their reading. I have found that junior children who think they are good at

Motte and Bailey

How and why castles were built?

Why were they built? They were built to keep attackers out and to keep Normans villagers safe. They kept slaves as well. They lived there as well.

How castles were built? First they made a mound which was very big then dug a ditch for the moat and the earth would make the motte. They then made a tower on the top of the mound. Then they made the inner bailey which is the fence around the tower and the outer bailey is the fence around the chapel and straw huts. They made a sort of ladder from the village to the tower. There is a small moat around the inner bailey. There was a drawbrigde to the outer bailey. They then were finished.

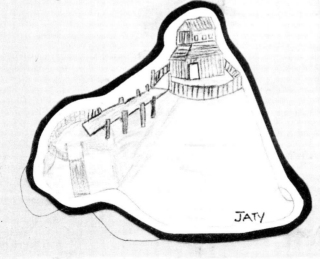

JATY

Fig. 8.24b

Motte and Bailey
Castles.

IMOGEN.

Motte and Bailey castles were built
on a motte so they could see
their attackers coming. The motte
would be dug out of mud and
moulded into a hill shape. The motte
was in the middle of a moat. The
moat would be used for washing
clothes and drinking from. To cross
the moat would be a wooden bridge.
On the hill was a tower made out
of wood. They would see their attackers
through little slits in the tower.
Around the tower would be a wooden
fence. To get to the tower there was
steps made out of wood. At the
bottom of hill, and inside the moat
would be a fence. Inside the fence
would be a chapel and kitchen and
sometimes other rooms. The wood
would come from trees. The Bailey
is the ground that the chapel and
kitchen are on.

Fig. 8.24c

Castles

Fist I would dig a ditch round my big piece of land. Then I would build a mound, and put a high fence with points on them round it. Inside the fence I would build huts and stables. Then I would build a motte (a motte being a large mound) with a watchtower on top of it, with a high fence that also... I would invite William the Conqueror round to my castle, and give him a nice dinner with roast pheasant and wine. We would on a table and sit on wooden chairs with flowers carved on them both (round the edge with one in the middle). I would entertain him with juggles and acrobats then we would go for a ride on some horses armour. We would gallop over the moors then go back to the castle.

Fig. 8.24d

drawing actually have great difficulty in adapting to the modelling task because it is like making a draft drawing. They often do not attend to the meaning of the text. If this problem persists and the good drawer takes too long over a model, I set a very strict time limit and give the child a torn or used piece of paper on which to draw their model.

If children are asked to model from each other's written work it helps the writers to see what important information they have missed out. Not being able to view their own writing from a reader's point of view is a common problem for immature writers. This activity is another use of the modelling technique.

Strengths of modelling

1   Modelling is suitable for any age range.

2   Very young children can learn the technique quickly.

3   The technique is very popular with both good and poor readers.

4   Very often the so-called poor readers are able to put in more relevant details than the fluent readers.

5   Modelling encourages real interaction with the text: readers must be trying to comprehend the text because it is not possible to model unless you understand.

6   The reader is active.

7   Modelling can be a window on the comprehension process. The model is one of the best available means of finding out how the process of comprehension works. The technique helps the teacher to see which children are not reading with understanding, and to identify their problems.

8   Modelling is particularly helpful for teachers of children whose first language is not English, because many of these children are able to pretend they can understand written text when in fact they do not. Bilingual readers can often impress their teachers when reading out loud – they can pronounce the words and put in the right stress and intonation. However, meaning escapes them.

9   Modelling is a useful tool for pupils throughout their lives.

10 If children use modelling for notemaking they can overcome the two most often-quoted problems of traditional notemaking: reorganisation of information and using their own words.

11 My work suggests that modelling helps children to develop more flexible reading strategies.

Problems with modelling
1 It takes time for older children to have the confidence to produce rough sketches rather than neat, careful art work.

2 It takes time for some children to realise that it is the content of the text rather than the drawing that matters.

3 Not all texts can be modelling.

Patterning

Patterning is a method of notemaking popularised by Tony Buzan (1974). It involves taking meaningful words from the text and putting them into a structure that 'explodes' from one concept in the middle of a page. Patterns are arrangements of information that do not follow a linear structure: the most important theme is positioned in the middle, and 'spokes' are added, with themes of diminishing importance on them as one moves away from the centre.

Thomas and Harri–Augstein (1976) have suggested that if adults devote enough time to learning how to pattern it is the most effective of all strategies. I have adapted this technique for children, and certainly some of them find it very helpful. However, some children take time to gain advantage from it.

I have found that patterning is most useful if combined with underlining: children select words from a text and then transfer them to a piece of paper, preferably as a list. The original piece of text is taken away, then on another piece of paper, with coloured pens, they use their words to create a pattern. Each strand of the pattern must be related to the core and each word on each strand must be placed so that the relationship with the rest of the strand is understood.

The great advantage is that every child's pattern will be different. As with modelling, the pattern must not be valued for itself: it is a working document and should be changed or crossed out freely. Although the patterns often look very attractive, and the children are proud of them, they must be treated as a form of notemaking and not as a finished product. Figure 8.25a and b opposite, show a typical pattern and the written work that the children produced from it.

Strengths of patterning

1   Patterning is suitable for all ages.

2   Patterning can be used on any text.

3   Slower children particularly, seem to blossom on this technique.

4   Patterning is a technique that is often easily acquired by young children.

5   Older children can add to their patterns when they read new texts on a topic. Hence when patterning is used as a form of notemaking, it is easy to combine the notes from different books.

6   Writing up from a pattern is usually a very quick process, because most of the hard work has already been done. (Sometimes I suggest to children that they number the branches so they know which bit of the writing to attack first. Each branch then becomes a paragraph.)

7   The resulting written work is usually well-structured and far superior to that which the children would normally produce.

Problems with patterning

1   Although it is easily picked up by young children, patterning is often more difficult for adults: they are used to thinking in a linear fashion and often find the 'exploding' concept difficult. I have found that adults are hesitant to try the strategy with their children.

2   Some children find the process takes too long.

3   Some children find the process too hard.

STRATEGIES THAT HELP CHILDREN LEARN FROM TEXTS

I have found some strategies do not necessarily lead to good notes, but do help to develop children's reading on informational texts. They help them to become active and to interact with the text.

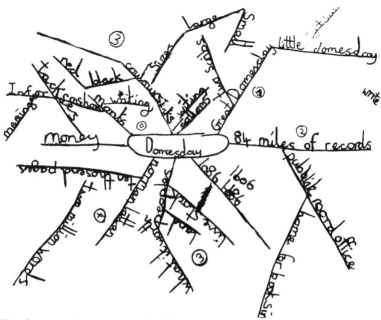

Fig. 8.25a   A nine-year-old child's pattern

Fig. 8.25b
Written work
produced
after
using the
patterns
for notes

King William and the Norman,
Orded some Monks to
Wright the great Domesday
kings book also know as the
great Domesday It had all
the informashon of the land
and how much it was worth so
king William would know how much
tax theyed have to pay. there is
Pubblic record office too it
holds the records for the
Domesday the record office has
it 84 miles of records, It has
been the home of it sence 1859
and it took 20 years to right
2 million words careffly riton. In the
writing of the Domesday
book it had four tipps
of ink there were two
coulours used were red
and black, To collked the
informshon william sent out

messingers, to get it.

Cut and match

This is a technique that I have developed myself. It requires either two copies of an old book that has no further use (two so that you can use both sides of each page) or photocopies of the relevant pages. The text and the illustrations are cut up and numbered. These are then laminated. The idea is that the children have to use their reading skills and their knowledge of the subject to arrange the text and illustrations into some semblance of order. The children work in pairs to work-out which piece of text goes with a particular illustration.

After the children have matched up the text and illustrations, they are asked to sequence them to see if they can find the original order. I have found that this technique works very well with information books that I have rejected because their language is too simple. If they have a historical theme it works even better, because the children have to use their knowledge of the chronology of events as well as trying to use the language of the text to see which piece of text goes where.

Strengths of cut and match
1   Children use their understanding of the text to work out which text goes with which illustration: each has to be studied in turn.

2   During the activity, children develop an understanding of cohesion. There will be some words in each piece of text that relate to another piece. Children can realise how connectives such as *however, although* or *consequently* join one piece of text to another.

3   When the children work in pairs this technique creates a lot of discussion.

4   Children are likely to work on one text for a considerable length of time: they will be reading and re-reading it.

5   Children really enjoy this activity: they feel important with all the pieces of paper. It is an advantage for some children that there is no writing involved.

6   Once the necessary equipment has been made it can be re-used.

Weaknesses of cut and match
1   Cut and Match activities can take a long time to prepare.

2   Storage is a problem: the pieces are best kept in envelopes.

Cut and label

This technique is similar to Cut and Match, but involves positioning labels on illustrations. The children are given a diagram, or an illustration with arrows or spaces where the labels should be, and a pile of labels or captions each on a separate piece of card. They then have to read the relevant text to find out where the appropriate labels go. The children have to search the text for meaning and to deduce which label matches which part of the illustration.

I have found this an immensely useful activity, because children do have to be taught how to analyse diagrams and illustrations. They are expected to learn from them but they are rarely given any guidance on how to do so. Also, many young children do not understand the functions of captions: this activity helps to explain their uses.

I often use this Cut and Label technique to assess how much the children have gained from another reading activity, or as a further development. The most successful activities have been those with unequal numbers of labels and arrows. For instance the example shown in figure 8.26a and b has 12 captions but 13 arrows. It is surprising how much more difficult the task is, if this challenge is added.

CONCLUSION

This book is about the way children learn, the way children read and the mismatch between these two demands and the child's books currently in schools. My hope is that you will now appreciate just how difficult some aspects of reading and learning are, that you will sympathise with your children in their attempts to extract new areas of knowledge from texts, and you will not allow them to reject informative texts altogether. To use the texts constructively they must be taught to be selective, critical and reflective readers. The techniques that I have discussed in the last chapter will help these skills to be developed and enhanced.

I have run courses and INSET days for teachers up and down the country on all the issues discussed in this book and a comment I frequently hear from the participants after the course is: 'Oh if only I had been taught this in my youth.' My hunch is that if children are taught these strategies early in their school career they will have them for life.

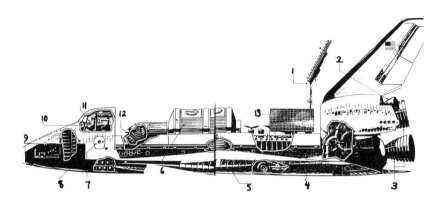

The wings front edges are designed to withstand temperatures of 1,570°C	Flight deck, houses the crew — a commander, pilot and another person	Two orbital manoeuvring engines - one on each side of the tail. They are used to move the space - plane in and out of orbit.
tunnel links living quarters to Spacelab	nose cap prevents against 1,260 °C re-entry heat.	Microwave radio scanner used for studying the ionosphere
Hatch to living quarters and flight deck. This has 4 bunk beds, toilets and washing facilities	The three main engines each give 213,000 kg maximum thrust. They burn for 8 minutes after the launch.	Platform on which scientific instruments are mounted.
The brickwork effect is caused by heat insulation tiles fixed to the outside	The main undercarriage is retracted into bay in the wing	A computer navigates and controls the plane

Fig. 8.26a and b The children were asked to match the individual cards with leader lines on the space shuttle

POSTSCRIPT

This book started on a note of failure. It ends, I hope, with enthusiasm for the future. The way forward for children's informative reading and writing is very exciting.

I worked with top juniors when I first started this research and, as was shown in the last chapter, I achieved very satisfactory results. However, I realised that by this age children have preconceived ideas about what reading and notemaking are, and that these take time to break down, so I thought it was worth trying to teach younger children. I then decided to start work with 7 and 8 year-olds. I had more immediate success here, so I then moved with a mixture of excitement and trepidation to the infants. This is where the work really took off.

Infants are inexperienced readers so they have few preconceptions of what informational reading is all about. Reading to learn and learning to read can be part of the same process for these young children. It seems from my work in schools that if the very young are exposed to the idea that there are different types of reading, then with support, they will continue to develop their reading strategies as they move up the school.

I have made reference to the close connection between reading and writing throughout this book, but here I must stress the importance of children appreciating these links. In my view it is only when children have to write in an informative manner that they realise the significance of notemaking and reading to learn. The most successful way to establish the links between reading and writing is to get young children to write for real audiences. If children try to write their own information books for a younger class, or for the school library, then they are actively using the strategies detailed in this book. The books written by children for each other tend to be very clear and to give the type of information that adults might leave out. Children seem to have a clear understanding of what other children will find interesting and what needs clarifying.

This leads me back to the main thrust of this book which is that we do not have enough good information books in our schools at the present time. Books are now being published with more structural guiders, and publishers are trying to make their books more readable. Even so, I do not feel they have got the message that very simple books do not make good information books, and nor do unnecessarily complex ones. Teachers should be demanding information books which are excellent models for children's writing, and which have the same features as a good adult information text. They should be demanding 'big books' for shared informational reading; taped information books for children to listen to;

dual language information books; resource packs with various text types; books which can be read at many different levels.

In today's classroom with its emphasis on shared reading and writing activities, it is important the sharing continues into the field of notemaking. Children and teachers can learn and experiment alongside each other. Large information books can be put on a stand and children can select which type of notemaking they might use for each section of text. Selection of text and choice of strategy can then be made in public with the children playing a leading rôle.

I hope that you have enjoyed reading this book and that you will go on to experiment with various ways of making notes and using informative texts. This type of work is only in its infancy and there is so much to learn. I look forward to hearing from schools who have worked hard in this area of the curriculum or from those who have experienced problems. I hope that teachers, librarians and any other interested adults who have read this book will become more confident with their own reading and will be able to use some of these skills not only with their children but in their own work as well.

Bibliography

ANDERSON, J. 1982 'The writer, the reader, and the text: or writhing, and reeling in texta.' Paper presented at UKRA conference, July 1982

ANDERSON, J. 1983 'The writer, the reader and the text' in B. Gilham (ed.) *Reading Through the Curriculum*, UKRA

ANDERSON, R. C. AND ANDERSON, M. C. 1978 *Schemata as Scaffolding for the representation of information in connected discourse* (Reading Education Report no. 24) Urbana: University of Illinois, Center for the Study of Reading

ANDERSON, R. C. AND DAVISON, A. 1986 *Conceptual and Empirical Bases of Readability Formulas* Urbana: University of Illinois, Center for the Study of Reading

ANDERSON, R. C., MASON, J. AND SHIRLEY, L. 1984 'The reading group: an experimental analysis of a labyrinth' *Reading Research Quarterly* 20, pp.6–38

ANDERSON, T. H. 1980 'Study Skills and Adjunct Aids' in R. J. Spiro, B. C. Bruce, and W. F. Brewer (eds.) *Theoretical Issues in Reading Comprehension*, Hillsdale, NJ, Erlbaum

ANDERSON, T. H., ARMBRUSTER, B. B. 1981 *Content Area Textbooks* (Reading Education Report no. 23) Urbana: University of Illinois, Center for the Study of Reading

ANDERSON, T. H., ARMBRUSTER, B. B. 1984 'Studying' in D. Pearson (ed.) *Handbook of Reading Research*, New York, Longman

ANDERSON, T. H., ARMBRUSTER, B. B. AND KANTOR, R. N. 1980 *How clearly Written are children's textbooks? Or of bladderworts and alfa* (Reading Education Report no. 16) Urbana: University of Illinois, Center for the Study of Reading

ARMBRUSTER, B. B. AND ANDERSON, T. H. 1982 *Idea Mapping: the Technique and its use in the classroom or simulating the ups and downs of reading Comprehension* (Reading Education Report no. 36) Urbana: University of Illinois, Center for the Study of Reading

ASSESSMENT OF PERFORMANCE UNIT 1982 *Language performance in Schools: Primary Survey Report no. 2* London, HMSO

ASSOCIATION FOR SCIENCE EDUCATION. 1989 *Report*, Hatfield, Herts, Association for Science Education

AUSUBEL, D. P. 1968 *Educational Psychology: A Cognitive View* New York, Holt, Rinehart & Winston

AUSUBEL, D. P. 1978 'In defense of advance organizers: A reply to the critics' *Review of Educational Research* 48, pp.251–7

AVON SCHOOLS. 1986 Issues 3 *Can a kangaroo jump?* Bristol

BAKER, L. 1978 'Processing temporal relationships in simple stories: effects of input sequence' *Journal of Verbal Learning and Verbal Behaviour* 17, pp.559–72

BANTON, W. E., AND SMITH, C. F. 1974 'Review of research on college adult reading' in A. H. McNinch and W. D. Muller (eds.) *Reading Convention and Inquiry 24th Yearbook* National Reading Conference, South Carolina

BAUM, A., AND INGHAM, J. 1983 'Into the classroom reading record forms' *Reading* 17, pp.161–70

BEREITER, C. March 1978 *Discourse Type Schema and Strategy – a View From the Standpoint of Instructional Design*, Paper presented at the American Educational Research Association meeting, Toronto

BEREITER, C. 1985 'Children need more complex reading strategies' in J. Osborn et al (ed.) *Reading Education: Foundations for a Literate America* D. C. Heath and Co. (From SCR Illinois)

BERKOWITZ, S. 1986 'Effects of instruction in text organisation on sixth grade students' memory for expository reading' *Reading Research Quarterly* 21, pp.161–77

BERRY, M. 1975 *Introduction to systemic linguistics: structures and systems* London, Batsford

BEVERTON, S. 1986 'Going into Secondary Reading' in B. Gillham (ed.) *The Language of School Subjects* London, Heinemann

BLIGH, J., CLOUDSLEY THOMPSON, J. C., MACDONALD, A. G., 1976 *Environmental Physiology of Animals*, Oxford, Blackwell Scientific Publications

BLOOM, W. 1985 'Information skills through project work' in P. Avann (ed.) *Teaching Information Skills in the Primary School* Sevenoaks, Edward Arnold

BRANSFORD, J. D. AND JOHNSON, M. K. 1972 'Contextual prerequisites for understanding. Some investigations of comprehension and recall' *Journal of Verbal Learning and Verbal Behaviour* 11, pp.717–26

BRIDGE, C. A. AND WINOGRAD, P. 1982 'Readers' awareness of cohesive relationships during close comprehension' *Journal of Reading Behaviour* XIV, pp.299–312

BROWN, A., DAY, J. AND JONES, R. 1983 *The Development of Plans for Summarising Text* (Technical report no. 268) Urbana: University of Illinois, Center for the Study of Reading

BRUNNER, J. AND CAMPBELL, J. 1976 *Participating in Reading: A Practical*

Approach Englewood Cliffs, NJ, Prentice-Hall

BULMAN, L. 1985 *Teaching Language and Study Skills in Secondary Schools* London, Heineman

BUZAN, T. 1974 *Use Your Head* London, BBC

CALFEE, R. AND CURLEY, R. 1984 'Structures of prose in the content areas' in J. Flood (ed.), *Understanding Comprehension* Newark, Delaware, International Reading Association

CAMPIONE, J. AND ARMBRUSTER, B. 1985 'Acquiring information from texts: an analysis of four approaches' in J. Segal, S. Chipman and R. Glaser (eds.) *Thinking and Learning Skills*, Hillsdale NJ, Lawrence Erlbaum Associates Inc

CARTER, B., AND HARRIS, K. 1982 'What junior high students like in books', *Journal of Reading* 26, pp.42–6

CASHDAN, A., AND GRUGEON, E. (ed.) 1972 *Language in Education: A Source Book prepared by the Language and Learning Course Team*, London, Routledge and Kegan Paul for the Open University

CENTRAL ADVISORY COUNCIL FOR EDUCATION, PLOWDEN, B. 1967 *Children and Their Primary Schools. A Report of the Central Advisory Council for England 1* London, HMSO

CHALL, J. 1958 *Readability – An Appraisal of Research and Application*, Columbus, Ohio Bureau of Educational Research, Ohio State University

CHALL, J. 1980 'Readability and prose comprehension; continuities and discontinuities' in J. Flood (ed.) *Understanding Reading Comprehension*, Newark, Delaware, International Reading Association

CHAPMAN, L. J. 1984 'Comprehending and the teaching of reading' in J. Flood (ed.) *Promoting Reading Comprehension* Newark, Delaware, International Reading Association, pp.261–72

CHAPMAN, L. J. AND HOFFMAN, M. 1976 'Reading Development Course. An informal reading inventory for use with 12 to 13 year olds'. *Developing Fluent Reading*, Milton Keynes, Open University Press

CHAPMAN, L. J. AND LOUW, W. 1986 'Register development and secondary school texts' in B. Gillham (ed.) *The Language of School Subjects*, London, Heinemann

CHARROW, R. P. 1988 'Readability versus comprehensibility: a case study in improving a real document' in A. Davison and G. Green (ed.) *Linguistic complexity and text Comprehension: Readability Issues Reconsidered*, Hillside NJ, Lawrence Erlbaum Associates Inc

CHARROW, R. P. AND CHARROW, V. R. 1979 'Making legal language understandable: a psycholinguistic study of jury instructions' *Law Review* 79, pp.1306–74

CHRISTIE, F. 1984 'The Functions of Language. Preschool Language Learning and the Transition to Print' in Geelong, *Language Studies Children Writing: A Reader* Deakin University, Australia

CHURCH, S. 1985 'Text Organisation: its value for literacy development' in J. Newman (ed.) *Whole Language Theory*, New York, Heinemann

COLE, P. AND GARDNER, J. 1981 *Radical Pragmatics*, New York, Academic Press

COLERIDGE, S. T. 1977 'Notebooks' as quoted by J. E. Merritt and D. Prior (eds.) in *Developing Independence in Reading* Milton Keynes, Open University

COMMITTEE OF INQUIRY INTO READING AND THE USE OF ENGLISH 1975 *A Language For Life*: report of the committee of inquiry appointed by the Secretary of State for Education and Science under the chairmanship of Sir Alan Bullock, London, HMSO

COOKE, G. 1978 *Studying – a practical guide for students of all ages*, London, National Youth Bureau

COX, C. B., AND BOYSON, K. 1977 *Black Paper*, London, Temple Smith

COX, C. B., AND DYSON, A. E. 1971 *Black Papers in Education*, London, Davis Poynter

CRISMORE, A. 1983 *Metadiscourse: What It Is and How It Is Used in School and Non-School Social Science Texts* (Technical report no. 273) Urbana: University of Illinois, Center for the Study of Reading

CRISMORE, A. 1980 *Student Use of Selected Formal Logical Connectors Across School Level and Type* Unpublished Paper. Indiana, Purdue University

CROUSE, P., AND IDSTEIN, D. 1972 'Effects of Encoding Cues on Prose Learning' *Journal of Educational Psychology* 63 pp.309–13

CRYSTAL, D. 1986 'Literacy 2000', *English Today*

DANSEREAU, D. 1982 *Utilising intact and embedded headings as processing aids with non-narrative texts* (ERIC document no. 218) Urbana: University of Illinois, Center for the Study of Reading

DANSEREAU, D., BROOKS, L. W., SPURLIN, J. E. AND HOLLEY, C. D. 1979 'Development and evaluation of an effective learning strategy programme', *Journal of Educational Psychology* 71 pp.64–73

DAVIES, D. 1985 'Introducing Information Skills in the Infant School' in P. Avanna (ed.) *Teaching Information Skills in the Primary School* Sevenoaks, Edward Arnold

DAVIES, F. 1986 *Books in the School Curriculum: A Report from the National Book league* London, The Publishers Association

DAVIES, F. AND GREENE, T. 1984 *Reading for Learning in the Sciences*, London, Oliver and Boyd

DAVISON, A. 1986 *Readability and Questions of Textbook Difficulty* (Reading Report no. 66), Urbana, University of Illinois, Center for the Study of Reading

DAVISON, D., KANTOR, R. N., HANNAH, J., HERMON, G., LUTZ, R. AND SALZILLO, R. 1980 *Limitations of Readability Formulas in Guiding Adaptations of Texts* (Technical Report no. 162), Urbana: University of Illinois, Center for the Study of Reading

DE BEAUGRANDE, R. 1980 *Text Discourse and Process Toward a Multi-disciplinary Science of Texts*, Norwood, NJ, Ablex

DEPARTMENT OF EDUCATION AND SCIENCE 1978 *Primary Education in England: The Report of a Survey by HMI of Schools*, London, HMSO

DEPARTMENT OF EDUCATION AND SCIENCE 1982 *Education 5 to 9: An illustrative Survey of Eighty First Schools in England*, London, HMSO

DEPARTMENT OF EDUCATION AND SCIENCE 1987 *The National Curriculum*, London, HMSO

DEPARTMENT OF EDUCATION AND SCIENCE 1989 *Reading Policy and Practice at Ages 5–14*, London, DES

DICKIE, G. 1975 'The Myth of the aesthetic attitude', in G. W. F. Hegel, *Hegel's Aesthetics*, Oxford, Oxford University Press

DONALDSON, M. 1988 *Sense and sensibility: Some thoughts on the teaching of literacy*, Occasional Paper no. 3, Reading and language information centre, Reading

DOOLING, D., AND LACHMAN, B. 1971 'Effects of Comprehension on Retension of Prose' *Journal of Experimental Psychology* 88 pp.216–22

ENGLISH, E. 1987 'The Design of Versatile Text Materials' *Open Learning*, Milton Keynes, Open University Press

ENGLISH MAGAZINE Autumn 1980 *Comprehension Part One*, Issue 5, London

ENGLISH MAGAZINE Autumn 1980 *Comprehension Part Two*, Issue 5, London

ENGLISH MAGAZINE Spring 1981 *Comprehension Part Three*, Issue 6, London

FISHER, M. 1972 *Matters of Fact*, Leicester, Brockhampton Press

FLOOD, J. 1986 'The Text, The Student and The Teacher: Learning From Exposition in Middle Schools', *The Reading Teacher* 39 pp.784–91

FOSTER, D. AND COLES, J. 1977 'An Experimental Study of Typographical Cueing in Printed Text' *Ergonomics* 20 pp.57–66

FOWLER, R. L., AND BARKER, A. S. 1974 'Effectiveness of highlighting for retention of material' *Journal of Applied Psychology* 59 pp.358–64

FRY, D. 1985 *Children Talk About Books: Seeing Themselves as Readers*, Milton Keynes, Open University Press

FYFE, R. AND MITCHELL, E. 1985 *Reading Strategies and Their Assessment* Slough, N. F. E. R. Nelson

GAGG, J. C. 16 Feb 1968 'The Sixteen Papers' in *The Times Educational Supplement* p.537

GEVA, E. 1983 'Facilitating Reading Comprehension Through Flow-charting' in *Reading Research Quarterly* 8, pp.384–405

GIBBS, G., MORGAN, A., AND TAYLOR, L. 1980 *Understanding why students don't learn* (Institute of Educational Technology: Study methods group report no. 5)

GILLHAM, B. 1986 *The Language of School Subjects*, London, Heinemann

GOETZ, B. AND ARMBRUSTER, B. 1980 'Psychological correlates of text structure' in R. Spiro, B. Bruce and J. Brewer (eds.) *Theoretical Issues in Reading Comprehension*, Hillsdale, NJ, Lawrence Erlbaum Associates, Inc

GOLDSTEIN, R., AND UNDERWOOD, G. 1981 'The Influence of Pictures on the Derivation of Meaning from Children's Reading Materials' *Journal of Research in Reading* 4 pp.6–16

GOODMAN, K. S. 1976 'Reading a Psycholinguistic Guessing Game' in H. Singer and R. Ruddell (eds.) *Theoretical Models and Processes of Reading* Newark Delaware, International Reading Association

GRAHAM, W. 1978 'Readability and Science Textbooks' in *School Science Review* pp.545–50

GREEN, M. G., AND OLSON, M. S., 'Preferences for and the comprehension of original and readability adapted materials' in A. Davison and G. Green (eds.) *Linguistic Complexity and Text Comprehension: Readability Issues Reconsidered*, 1988, Hillsdale, New Jersey, Lawrence Erlbaum Associates Inc

GRELLET. F. 1981 *Developing Reading Skills* Cambridge University Press

HAGBERG, J. 1975 'Making the right to read in the content areas a reality' in B. Smith and J. Schulwitz, *Teacher Tangible Techniques, Comprehension of Content in Reading*, Hillsdale, NJ, Lawrence Erlbaum Associates Inc

HAHNEMANN, S., 1952, *Organon of Medicine*, Boericke and Tafel

HALLIDAY, M. A. K. 1973 *Explorations in the Function of language* London, Edward Arnold

HALLIDAY, M. A. K. 1975 *Learning How to Mean*, London, Edward Arnold

HALLIDAY, M. A. K. 1978 *Language as Social Semiotic*, London, Edward Arnold

HALLIDAY, M. A. K., AND HASAN, R. 1976 *Cohesion in English*, London, Longman

HALLIDAY, M. A. K. AND HASAN, R. 1980 'Text and Context: Aspects of Language in a semi-semiotic Perspective' in *Sophia Linguistica Working Papers in Linguistics* VI The Graduate school of Languages and Linguistics, Tokyo, Japan

HARRIS, A. J. AND SIPAY, E. 1975 *How to Increase Reading Ability*, New York, McKay

HARRISON, C. 1980 *Readability in the Classroom*, Cambridge University Press

HASAN, R. 1980 'The texture of a text' in *Sophia Linguistica Working Papers in Linguistics* VI The Graduate school of Languages and Linguistics, Tokyo pp.43–59

HEATHER, P. 1984 'Teaching methods and the use of books and libraries in the primary school: a Review' *CRUS Occasional Paper* no. 11

HEEKS, P. 1981 *Choosing and Using Books in the First School*, London, Macmillan

HEEKS, P. 1982 *Ways of Knowing*, London, Signal Books

HERBER, H. 1970 *Teaching Reading in the Content Areas* Englewood Cliffs, NJ, Prentice-Hall

HOLDAWAY, D. 1979 *The Foundations of Literacy*, Auckland, New Zealand, Ashton Scholastic

HOUNSELL, D. AND MARTIN, E. 1980 *Using Books and Libraries Project*, Centre for Educational Research and Development, University of Lancaster

HULL, R. 1976 'The Language Gap' in R. Booth (ed.) *Preventing Difficulties in Learning*, London, Blackwell

IDSTEIN, P., AND JENKINS, J. R. 1972 'Underlining versus repetitive reading' *Journal of Educational Research* 65, pp.321–3

INGHAM, J. AND BROWN, V. 1986 *The State of Reading*, London, The Publishers' Association

IRVING, A. 1982 *Starting to Teach Study Skills*, Sevenoaks, Edward Arnold

IRVING, A. AND SNAPE, W. 1978 *Educating Library Users in Secondary Schools* British Library Research and Development Report No. 5467

IRWIN, J. W. 1983 'Coherence Factors in Children's Textbooks' *Reading Psychology* 4 pp.11–23

JANSEN, M. 1983 *Language and Concepts*, Paper presented at IRA conference

JANSEN, M. 1987 *Little About Language, Words and Concepts – Or What May Happen When Children Learn to Read*, Denmark. Landsforeningen af Laesepaedagogen

JENKINS, D., AND BAILEY, T. 1964 'Cue selection and mediated transfer in paired associated learning' *Journal of Experimental Psychology* 67, pp.101–2

KILPATRICK, A., MCCALL, P., AND PALMER, S. 1982 *See What You Mean*, London, Oliver and Boyd

KINTSCH, W. 1982 'Text representations' in W. Otto and S. White (eds.) *Reading Expository Material*, New York, Academic Press

KINTSCH, W., AND VAN DIJK, T. A. 1978 'Toward a model of text comprehension and production' *Psychology Review* 85 pp.363–94

KLARE, G. R. 1976 'A second look at the validity of readability formulas', *Journal of Reading Behaviour*, 8 pp.129–52

KLARE, G. R. 1974–5 'Assessing readability' *Reading Research Quarterly* 10 pp.62–102

KRESS, G. 1982 *Learning to Write* London, Routledge and Kegan Paul

LANGER, J. 1981 'Pre-reading plan PReP facilitating text comprehension' in (ed.) Chapman L. J. *The Reader and the Text* London, Heinemann

LAVENDER R. 1983 'Children using information books' *Education 3–13* pp.8–12

LITTLEFAIR, A. 1990 *Reading All Types of Writing*, Milton Keynes, Open University Press

LUNZER, E., AND GARDNER, K. (eds.) 1979 *The Effective Use of Reading*, London, Heinemann

LUNZER, E., GARDNER, K., DAVIES, F., AND GREENE, T. 1984 *Learning From the Written Word*, London, Oliver and Boyd

MANPOWER SERVICES COMMISSION, 1988 *Ensuring Quality in Open Learing – A Handbook for Action*, London Manpower Services Commission

MARK, J. 1976 *Thunder and Lightnings*, Harmonsworth, Puffin Books

MARLAND, M. 1982 'Information skills in the secondary school curriculum' *School Council Curriculum Bulletin no. 9*, London

MARTIN, B., AND BUCK, J. 1984 *Bridging the Gap between Primary and Secondary School*, (Inset Project Pack) Loughborough University

MARTIN, J. R. 1984 'Language register and genre' in Geelong (ed.) *Children Writing: Study Guide*, Deakin University, Australia

MCANDREW, D. A. November 1983 'Underlining and notetaking: some suggestions from research' *Journal of Reading*, pp.103–8

MCCALISTER, J. October 1964 'Using paragraph clues as aids to understanding', *Journal of Reading*, 8, pp. 11–16

MCCLURE, E., MASON, J., AND BARNITZ, J. 1979 'An exploratory study of story structure and age effects on children's ability to sequence stories' *Discourse Processes* 2. pp.213–49

MCDONALD, G. E. 1978 *The effects of instruction in the use of abstract structural schema as an aid to instruction and recall of written discourse*, (Unpublished doctoral dissertation) Virginia Polytechnic, Institute and State University

MCKENZIE, M., AND WARLOW, A. 1977 *Reading Matters: Selecting and Using Books in the Classroom*, London, Hodder and Stoughton in association with ILEA

MCLAUGHLIN, G. H. 1966 'Comparing Styles of Presenting Technical Information' *Ergonomics* 9 pp.257–9

MEEK, M. 1982 *Learning to Read*, London, Bodley Head

MERRITT, J. 1978 'Learning to read and reading to learn; developing effective reading' in E. Hunter-Grundin and H. Grundin (eds.) *Reading: Implementing the Bullock Report*, London, Ward Lock

MEYER, B. J. F. 1977 'The structure of prose effects on learning and memory and implications for educational practice' in R. C. Anderson, R. J. Spiro, W. E. Montague, (eds.) *Schooling and the Acquisition of Knowledge*, Hillsdale, NJ, Lawrence Erlbaum Associates Inc

MEYER, B. J. F. 1984 'Organizational aspects of text; effects on reading comprehension and applications for the classroom' in J. Flood (ed.) *Promoting Reading Comprehension*, Newark, Del., IRA

MEYER, B. J. F., BRANDT, O. M., AND BLUTH, G. J. 1980 'Use of top-level structure in text: key for reading comprehension of ninth grade students' *Reading Research Quarterly* 1 pp.72–103

MOBLEY, M. 1987 *Evaluating Curriculum Materials, Unit 2: Readability*, London, Longman

MORRIS, A. AND STEWART-DORE, N. 1984 *Learning To Learn From Text: ERICA Effective Reading in the Content Areas*, North Ryde NSW, Addison Wesley

MOY, B., AND RALEIGH, M. 1983 'Reading For Information Parts One and Two', English Magazine reprinted in Simons, M. and Plackett, E. (eds.) *The English Curriculum: Reading 1 Comprehension*, The English Centre, London

NATIONAL CURRICULUM COUNCIL, March 1989 *National Curriculum Council Consultation Report*, York, National Curriculum Council

NELSON, K. 1978 The Syntagmatic–Pardigmatic Shift Revisited. A review of Research and Theory. Psychology Review 84 pp.93–116

NEWTON, L. 1983 'The Effect of Illustrations' *Reading* 17 pp.43–55

NISBET, J., AND SHUCKSMITH, J. 1986 *Learning strategies*, London, Routledge and Kegan Paul

ORLANDO, V. P. 1979 'The Relative Effectiveness of a Modified Version of SQ3R on University Students Study Behaviour', An unpublished study thesis, Pennsylvannia

ORNA, E. 1985 'The author: help or stumbling block on the road to designing usable texts' in T. M. Duffy and R. Waller (eds.) *Usable Texts*, New York, Academic Press

OSBORN, J. ET AL 1985 *Reading Education: Foundations for a Literate America* D. C. Heath and Co. (from CSR in Illinois)

OTTO, W., AND WHITE, S. 1982 *Reading Expository Material*, New York, Academic Press

PAICE, S. Spring 1984 'Reading to Learn' *English in Education*, 18 pp.3–9

PEARSON, P. D., HANSEN, J., AND GORDON, C. 1979 'The effect of background knowledge on young children's comprehension of explicit and implicit information; *Journal of Reading Behaviour* 11 pp.201–210

PEARSON, P. D., AND JOHNSON, D. D. 1978 *Teaching Reading Comprehension*, New York, Holt, Rinehart and Winston

PERERA, K. 1979 'The language demands of school learning' *Supplementary reading for Block 6 Open University Course P 232 Language Development*, Milton Keynes, Open University Press

PERERA, K. 1981 'Some language problems in school learning' in N. Mercer (ed.) *Language in School and Community*, Sevenoaks, Edward Arnold

PERERA, K. 1984 *Children's Writing and Reading*, London, Blackwell

PERERA, K. 1986(a) 'Grammatical differentiation between speech and writing in children aged 8 to 12' in A. Wilkinson (ed.) *The Writing of Writing*, Milton Keynes, Open University Press

PERERA, K. 1986(b) 'Some linguistic difficulties in school textbooks' in B. Gillham (ed.) *The Language of School Subjects*, London, Heinemann

PERERA, K. 1987 'Understanding language' in N. Mercer (ed.) *Language and Literacy in school from an educational perspective* 2 Milton Keynes, Open University Press

PILCHER, R. 1987 *The Shell Seekers*, Sevenoaks, Hodder and Stoughton

PUGH, A. K. 1978 *Silent Reading: An Introduction to its Study and Teaching* London, Heinemann

QUADLING, D. 17 January 1981 'A Conspiracy of Difficulty' *Times Educational Supplement*

QUIRK, GREENBAUM, LEECH, AND SVARTVIK, 1972 *A Grammar of Contemporary English*, Harlow, Longman

RALEIGH, M. 1981 'Special kinds of writing' *The Languages Book*, London, ILEA

REIGELUTH, C., AND STEIN, F. 1983 'The elaboration theory of instruction' in C. Reigeluth (ed.) *Instructional Design Theories and Models: An Overview of Their Current Status*, Hillsdale, NJ, Lawrence Erlbaum Associates Inc

ROBINSON, F. P. 1962 *Effective Reading*, New York, Harper and Row

ROE, B. D., STOODT, B. D., AND BURNS, P. C. 1978 *Reading Instruction in the Secondary School*, Chicago, Rand McNally

RODGERS, D. 1974 'Which connectives?' *Journal of Reading* 17(6) pp.462–6

ROSEN, H. 1972 'The language of textbooks' in A. Cashdan and E. Grugeon (eds.) *Language in Education; A Source Book prepared by the Language and*

Learning Course Team, 1972 Routledge and Kegan Paul for the Open University, London

ROSS, A. 1982 *Social Studies Occasional Paper 1* London, ILEA

ROTHERY, A. 1986 'Readability in maths' in B. Gillham (ed.) *The Language of School Subjects*, London, Heinemann

ROTHERY, J. 1980 *Working Papers in Linguistics. Writing Project no 1*, Linguistic Department, University of Sydney

ROTHERY, J. 1984 'The Development of genres – primary to junior secondary school' in Geelong (ed.) *Language Studies: children writing: study guide*, Australia, Deakin University Press

ROTHKOPT, E. Z. 1965 'Some theoretical and experimental approaches to problems in written instructions' in B. Krumboltz (ed.) *Learning and The Educational Process* Chicago, Rand McNally

ROTHKOPT, E. Z. 1982 'Adjunct aids and the control of mathemagenic activities during purposeful reading' in W. Otto and S. White (eds.) *Reading Expository Material*, New York, Academic Press

ROWNTREE, D. (ed.) 1988 *Ensuring Quality in Open learning A handbook for Action*, England, Manpower Services Commission

SANFORD, A. J., AND GARROD, S. C. 1981 *Understanding Written Language*, New York, Wiley

SCHALLERT, D. L. 1975 *Improving Memory for Prose: The relationship between depth of processing and content*, (Technical Report no. 5), Urbana: University of Illinois, Center for the Study of Reading

SCHALLERT, D. L., AND KLEINMAN, G. M. 1979 *Why the teacher is easier to understand than the textbook*, (Reading Education Report no. 9), Urbana: University of Illinois, Center for the Study of Reading

SCHWARTZ, R. M. 1975 *Levels of Processing: The Strategic Demands of Reading Comprehension* (August no. 135), Urbana: University of Illinois, Center for the Study of Reading

SHIMMERLIK, S. M., AND NOLAN, J. D. 1976 'Reorganisation and the recall of prose, *Journal of Educational Psychology* 68 pp.779–86

SMITH, F. 1972 *Understanding Reading* New York, Holt, Rinehart & Winston

SPIRO, R. J. 1980 'Constructive processes in prose comprehension and recall' in R. J. Spiro, B. C. Bruce and W. F. Brewer (eds.) *Theoretical Issues in Reading Comprehension*, Hillsdale, NJ, Lawrence Erlbaum Associates Inc

SPIRO, R. J., AND TAYLOR, B. M. 1980 *On Investigating Transition From Narrative to Expository Discourse: The Multidimensional Nature of Psychological Text Classifications* (Technical Report no. 195), Urbana: University of Illinois, Center for the Study of Reading

STORDAHL, K. E., AND CHRISTENSTEIN, C. M. 1956 'The effect of study techniques in comprehension and retension' *Journal of Educational Research* 46 pp.3–11

SUPRAMANIAM, S., AND BEARD, R. 1983 *Beyond Fluent Reading to comprehension*, (Supplementary Unit for Course PE231: Reading Development), Milton Keynes, Open University

SUTTON, C. 1981 (ed.) *Communicating in the Classroom*, London, Hodder and Stoughton

TANN, S. 1987 'Topic work: A mismatch of perceptions; *Reading* 21 pp.62–70

TANN, S. 1988 *Developing Topic Work in the Primary School*, Lewes, Falmer Press

TANN, S., AND BEARD, R. 26th May 1989 'Required Reading', *Times Educational Supplement*

TAYLOR, K. 1986 'Summary writing by young children' *Reading Research Quarterly*, Spring pp.193–209

THOMAS, L., AND HARRI-AUGSTEIN, S. 1976 *The self organised learner and the printed word* (a report to the social science Research Council) Uxbridge, Brunel University Centre for the Study of Human Learning

THORNTON, G. 1986 *APU Language Testing 1979–1983 An independent Appraisal of the Findings*, London, DES

TIERNEY, R., AND MOSENTHAL, J. 1980 *Discourse Comprehension and Production: Analysing Text Structure and Cohesion* (Technical Report no. 152) Urbana: University of Illinois, Center for the Study of Reading

TIERNEY, R., MOSENTHAL, J., AND KANTOR, R. 1984 'Classroom application of text analysis; towards improving text selection and use' in *Promoting Reading Comprehension*, J. Flood (ed.) Newark, Delaware, International Reading Association

TORBE, M., AND MEDWAY, P. 1981 *The Climate for Learning*, London, Ward Lock Educational

TONJES, M. J. 1986 'Reading and thinking skills required in the subject classroom' in B. Gillham (ed.), *The Language of School Subjects*, London, Heinemann

WALKER, C. 1974 *Reading Development and Extension*, London, Ward Lock Educational

WATKINS, A. E. 1979 'The symbols and mathematical structures of mathematical English and the reading comprehension of college students' *Journal of Research in Mathematical Education* 10 pp.216–18

WHITEHEAD, F. 1977 *Children and Their Books*, (Schools' Council Research Project on Children's Reading Habits), London, Macmillan

WHYSALL, R. 1987 'Reading for Information in the Primary School' *Reading* 21 pp.169–77

WILLIAMS, R. 1983 'A publisher's attempt to make its content–field textbooks more readable: a case study in social studies' in B. Gillham (ed.), *Reading Through the Curriculum* UKRA

WISHART, E. 1986 'Reading and Understanding History Textbooks; in B. Gillham (ed.) *The Language of School Subjects*, London, Heinemann

WRAY, D. 1985 *Teaching Information Skills Through Project Work*, Sevenoaks, Hodder and Stoughton in association with UKRA

WRIGHT, D. March 1987 'Books about countries', *Books For Keeps* 43, pp.6–7

List of project books mentioned in this book

A Wrigley Book About Time, D. Wrigley, Lutterworth Press, 1976
The Observer's Book of Mosses and Liverworts, A. Jewell, Frederick Warne, 1955
British Castles, A. Sorrell, Batsford, 1973
Everyday Life in Ancient Rome, Cowell, Batsford, 1961
Pompeii, Andrews, Cambridge University Press, 1978
Nature Reserves and Wildlife, Duffey, Heinemann, 1974
Rivers, M. Slack, Mills and Boon, 1985
Water and Weather, Updegraff, Methuen, 1986
The Greek and Roman World, J. Nicholl, Blackwell, 1983
The Story of Roman Britain, D. Baker, Edward Arnold, 1963
Icebergs, R. Gans, A. & C. Black, 1985
The Giraffe, Zebra Books, 1985
In Your Garden, R. Ainsworth, Heinemann, 1969
Explorers of the Nile, Langley, Wayland, 1981
Explorer's Guide – Trees, Chinery, Franklin Watts, 1980
The Romans and Their Empire, T. Cairns, Cambridge University Press, 1972
Easy Sweetmaking, D. Cox, Chatto and Windus, 1975
Purnell's Animals of Europe, M. Pia and A. Minelli, Purnell, 1984
Eggs, L. Hinds, Franklin Watts, 1968
The Book of the House, Carpi (ed.), Benn, 1978
How they lived in a Roman Fort, I. Thomas, Lutterworth Press, 1983
Time, H. Kurth, Hart-Davis, 1977
Hides and Seekers, National Trust, 1979
The Cornfield, V. Luff, A. & C. Black, 1978
How They Lived in a Medieval Castle, Adams, Lutterworth Press, 1983
Water, A. Leutscher, Methuen, 1983
The Mushroom, G. Ingves, A. & C. Black, 1983
Things That Grow, H. Pluckrose, Franklin Watts, 1975
Tell Me The Time, L. Bradbury, Ladybird, 1981

Index

References in bold type are to figures

Author Index

MORE ABOUT FINDING OUT ABOUT FINDING OUT

Look out for Bobbie Neate's new publication *More About Finding Out About Finding Out* (proposed title) which is a development of this text and in line with recent initiatives including the National Literacy Strategy.

It is to be produced by SAGE Publications, 6 Bonhill Street, London EC2A 4PU (0171 374 0645, website: http://www.sagepub.co.uk) in the year 2000.

In this publication there will be reports on children using computer programs and CD ROMs. There will be plenty of ideas to help children write in different genres especially explanations and reports. With more specific classroom ideas to help teach young children notemaking, it will really help them read for understanding.

More classroom research will be included and a chapter will be devoted to the successes and problems of teaching children to use non-fiction in the Literacy Hour. There will also be more critical analysis on recently published information books for children and guidance on what to look for in good quality big information books and texts for guided reading.

The *Longman Book Project* is an educational resource which has been published as a result of the research which was reported on *Finding Out About Finding Out*. It consists of a series of topic books for children which are specifically written to help them read for information and make notes. They are accompanied by teachers' books and copymasters.

These can be obtained from Longman, Edinburgh Gate, Harlow, Essex. CM20 2JE - 0800 579 579.